The Accent of Success

A Practical Guide for International Students

ERIC SHIRAEV

GERALD L. BOYD

Prentice
Hall

Upper Saddle River, New Jersey 07458

Library of Congress Cataloging-in-Publicatiion Data

Shiraev, Eric, 1960-
  The accent of success : a practical guide for international students
Gerald L. Boyd.
    p. cm.
  Includes bibliographical references and index.
  ISBN 0-13-086617-2
    1. Students, Foreign—United States—Handbooks, manuals, etc.   2. Student
  adjustment—United States—Handbooks, manuals, etc.   3. Cross-cultural
  orientation—United States—Handbooks, manuals, etc.   I. Boyd, Gerald L.   II Title.

  LB2376.4 .S55 2001
  371.826'91—dc21
                                                                    00-032410

Acquisitions Editor: Sande Johnson
Assistant Editor: Michelle Williams
Production: Holcomb Hathaway
Director of Manufacturing and Production: Bruce Johnson
Managing Editor: Mary Carnis
Manufacturing Manager: Ed O'Dougherty
Art Director: Marianne Frasco
Marketing Manager: Jeff McIlroy
Marketing Assistant: Barbara Rosenberg
Cover Design Director: Jayne Conte
Cover Illustration: Jose Ortega, SIS/Images.com
Composition: Aerocraft Charter Art Service
Printing and Binding: R. R. Donnelley, Harrisonburg

Prentice-Hall International (UK) Limited, *London*
Prentice-Hall of Australia Pty. Limited, *Sydney*
Prentice-Hall Canada Inc., *Toronto*
Prentice-Hall Hispanoamericana, S.A., *Mexico*
Prentice-Hall of India Private Limited, *New Delhi*
Prentice-Hall of Japan, Inc., *Tokyo*
Pearson Education Singapore Pte. Ltd.
Editora Prentice-Hall do Brasil, Ltda., *Rio de Janeiro*

10 9 8 7 6 5 4 3 2 1
ISBN 0-13-086617-2

Contents

PART ONE FIRST THINGS   1

Chapter 1 *Colleges in the United States*   *3*

Selecting a school: American higher education. Public and private schools. What does "major" mean? Two-year and four-year colleges. Grades and credits. Transfer of credits. The application package. How to apply. Tuition and fees. Visa and visa status. How to apply and get your American visa.

Chapter 2 *Newcomer's Checklist*   *25*

What you have to know at the beginning. Inspection. School requirements. Counseling on campus and how to get help. Maintaining your visa status in America. American money. Credit cards. Social security number. Driver's license. Work permit. Public transportation and cars. Health and other types of insurance. Phone calls. Your access to the Internet. Basic things you have to know about American law.

Chapter 3 *Overcoming Culture Shock*   *39*

Understanding your own culture shock. The tribulations of nostalgia. Loss of control and status. The language barrier. Being different and looking different. Food, clothes, cars, and customs in America. Do Americans have different values? How to manage culture shock. How to explain your adjustment problems to yourself. How to change your thinking and accept the reality around you. How to form a new attitude and manage your expectations. How to make new things familiar and learn from others.

PART TWO STRATEGIES FOR SUCCESSFUL STUDENTS   63

Chapter 4 *Communicating with Professors*   *65*

Different styles of teaching. How to communicate successfully. How to talk to your professor. Email and telephone. Bringing gifts. Professors and your personal life. Rules of address. Can a student negotiate a grade? Rules of making and keeping appointments. Helpful tips about your resume. Looking for help: when you should and when you should not.

Chapter 5 *Tips for Writing*   87

How to take notes and write essays. Facts and opinions. How to improve your understanding. Practical exercises. Elements of critical thinking or how to be amused by ordinary things. Logical mistakes, cognitive errors, and self-made obstacles. How to prepare a plan for your paper and organize your time. The structure of the paper. How to cooperate with friends without cheating. What is plagiarism? Academic integrity and copyright.

PART THREE NEGOTIATING AMERICAN CULTURE   113

Chapter 6 *Culture*   115

What is American culture: diversity and tolerance. Geographic regions. A brief tour of United States history. How the U.S. government works. Civil rights. Individuals and society. Social institutions. Literature, poetry, music, sports, and other major achievements.

Chapter 7 *Gender Roles*   129

Gender roles in America: surveys and polls. Job and the family. Marriage in America. Gender stereotypes. Equality and discrimination. Affirmative action. Sexual harassment on campus. Sex culture.

Chapter 8 *Ethnicity, Race, Religion, and Adjustment*   147

Ethnicity, race, and nationality. Stereotyping: its nature and ways of reducing. Some religious holidays. Religion on campus: how to communicate your religious beliefs and customs. The nature of ethnic and religious tolerance and mutual respect.

Chapter 9 *Media*   167

Mass media and business. Popularity ratings. Talk shows, dramas, and sitcoms in your education. Television, news, and politics. Sports on television and your vocabulary. Newspapers, books, films, and the learning process. How to use newspapers for your home projects. Books as reference sources. Movies from an educational standpoint: what do we learn from them about America and Americans? How to use the Internet as a reference source.

Preface

In a way, we are all strangers. Very few of us stay in one place. We all come from somewhere. We move looking for knowledge, better lives, better opportunities, and new challenges. We are searching for peace, love, happiness, and freedom. We want to travel and explore. We try to find professions and occupations suited for our needs, skills, and talents. No matter what makes and motivates you to study in the United States—a long-planned and awaited journey or a sudden occasion—you are taking a decisive step in your life.

To be successful in college is not easy. It is especially tough if you are new to this country. The language, the customs, the rules, the weather—everything could become a new hurdle for you. There are many questions that can confuse any student. What is the correct visa? How do I choose the right college? What is the right program for me? How do I take notes in class? How do I get help? What shall I watch on television? How can I remain optimistic? This book addresses these and many other questions and problems that almost every foreign student will face on a college campus.

This book will help you overcome the initial myths and fears related to visas and will help you understand higher education in the United States. It also advises how to plan your day and how to get the most from the printed sources around you. It discusses how to organize your semester, make appointments, and plan ahead. It gives tips on how and where to talk to your professor. It trains you in productive note taking and essay writing. The book provides you with basic tools of critical thinking. It shows how to use American television, newspapers, and the Internet more effectively for your education. It will help you to understand American customs. From this book you will learn more about American conversations and greetings, celebrations and holidays, eating habits and shopping.

Once you make the decision to study in the United States, you will find that many advisors will emerge who have your best interests at heart. Listen to their advice, but make sure that you base your decisions on solid evidence. Let your decisions be informed by your own careful research. Once you have made a commitment to an institution, you should follow the process that the school presents to you and be timely in meeting your deadlines. Once you arrive in the United States, take advantage of the resources available at your college or university.

A companion website is available for this book:

www.prenhall.com/success

Throughout this book, the web symbol, at left, will indicate when topics are explored in more detail on the website.

We hope this book will steer you in the right directions. Remember that this will be a unique opportunity, so take responsibility for making it a productive and positive one. Good luck in your journey!

A note for students and advisors

Advising students in the area of visas related to education is a complicated process. People who are not qualified to give advice in this area often give students conflicting or confusing information. The Foreign Student Advisor at the school you attend should be fully trained, and you should follow his or her advice.

A professional association represents advisors; it is called the National Association of Foreign Student Advisors (NAFSA). This organization provides information, training, and resources for Foreign Student Advisors. Much of what is presented in this book that is related to visas was either directly or indirectly influenced by the NAFSA *Manual* and the U.S. Department of State *Code of Federal Regulations.* Information about NAFSA can be found on the Internet at www.nafsa.org.

Remember, however, that ultimately the U.S. Department of State issues visas and the Immigration and Naturalization Service grants status and permits entry into the United States. It is their rules and regulations to which we must adhere.

Acknowledgments

The authors would like to acknowledge the following people for their contributions to this textbook. In particular, we would like to thank Thomas Butler, John Ehle, Barbara Saperstone, Jeanne Morse, and Belle Wheelan, for their relentless support of a multicultural educational environment and our professional efforts. For help in the development of this book the authors would like to acknowledge Mary O'Neill and Kathy Lloyd, who have collaborated with us many times and have given us valuable advice on various topics. Many thanks go to our NVCC colleagues Florine Greenberg, Don Devers, Maurice L'Heureux, Elizabeth Tebow, Michelle Lewis, and Pam Stewart. We would also like to show appreciation to Mary Brooks (Eastern Washington University), Allison Rice (Hunter College), Dave Sperling (ESLcafe.com), Herbert Pierson (St. John's University), and Sergei Tsytsarev (Hofstra University) for their important contributions and insights. We gratefully acknowledge the helpful advice of David Levy (Pepperdine University) and Cheryl Koopman (Stanford University). A special note of appreciation is due to Michelle Williams and Sande Johnson at Prentice Hall, Gay Pauley at Holcomb Hathaway, and Sue Bierman for their professionalism and personal courtesy.

DEDICATION

To John and Judy Ehle,
Maria Grieg, Patricia Beckett, and Kay Haverkamp,
who opened doors for us.

The Accent of Success

A Practical Guide for International Students

Part One
First Things

Y ou have made a very important life decision: you want to travel to the United States to study. Let us begin with the simple question: What are your educational goals? The answer, of course, will vary from individual to individual. Some people may want to come to the United States to study the English language. Some want to pursue a four-year degree at a university. Others want to earn the highest academic degree they can. Deciding on your goal will help you to choose what you want to study and will help you to select the best school in the geographic area you like. This is easier said than done. From the moment you decide to study in the United States until you attend the very first lecture, there are many things to do. Applying to a school and getting the proper paperwork done is a very complicated process. But wait! Acceptance to a college or university is just the beginning of your journey. After you arrive in America, you will realize that there are millions of issues, large and small, that you will need to address! For many, study abroad is like beginning a new life. Isn't that important enough to prepare for such an exciting journey?

Chapter 1

Colleges in the United States

The following is a scenario that is very familiar to the authors of this text and exemplifies the misconception that people have about coming to the United States to study. The myth is that you can quickly run through a "grocery list" of things to do, and then hop on a plane and come to the United States to study. It is much more complicated than that, and those that take short cuts end up paying extra in time and money for their haste.

My home telephone rang late in the evening. It was a long-distance caller, a son of my good old friend, dialing from the other side of the planet to apologize for such a late intrusion and to tell me that he had finally made a decision to study in the U.S. "Have you already applied for a particular school?" I asked. "No." He replied. "Did you choose a school?" "No." "Do you want to apply for an ESL program first?" "I don't know." "Do you know how much it will cost?" "Not exactly." "Do you realize that it is too late to apply for the fall?" "No. I thought in America you don't have to wait or do this paperwork." "Listen," I finally told him, "I will send you an email about what to do and how to apply for school in the United States. However, be prepared to become a student in a year and a half, not earlier." "I am sorry," he interrupted me. "May I arrive on a tourist visa and then get into college? It will be easier for me." Now it was my turn to say "no."

SELECTING A SCHOOL

A great deal of planning needs to be done before making the decision to study here. The United States is a country with well over 3,000 colleges and universities, so one of the first steps involved in preparation is to decide which school you would like to attend. You may have a particular city or region in mind where you would like to study or a very specific educational program in which you are interested. Your decisions should be made thoughtfully and carefully. Many people have wasted valuable time and money by selecting the wrong institution for their educational goals. It is important to do some productive research for yourself. Many college guides are available in book form and on the World Wide Web (WWW) that provide detailed descriptions about colleges and some even rate the schools. Some popular titles are listed in Appendix 1.

Check the libraries in your community and local colleges or universities to see if they have copies available. If college guidebooks cannot be obtained locally, or if they are outdated, then buy a copy. Most of these titles retail for under $20.00 and are well worth the investment to have at least one.

Numerous websites serve as sources for college reviews. For example, most search engines like *Lycos*, *Altavista*, and *Yahoo* have links to review sites or they can connect you to a list of sites. In addition, most institutions have their own websites. When you are looking up colleges on the Web, keep in mind that websites serve not only as sources of information but also as marketing tools. Therefore, you should talk to as many people as you can to get a balanced profile of a particular school. Sometimes a personal reference can be more valuable and accurate than the printed materials sent out by the school. However, be careful not to allow one good or bad experience from another student to determine your overall opinion. Always try to get at least a second, third, or fourth judgment before making a decision.

TYPES OF POSTSECONDARY SCHOOLS

It is often said that there is a college or university for everyone in the United States, and this is very close to being true. As indicated earlier, the United States has well over 3,000 colleges and universities, ranging from very large research universities to very small liberal arts colleges. Any one of these might be best suited for a given student depending on his or her personal goals. There is no standard model that all colleges or universities follow; however, there are some general categories based on the kinds of degrees students can earn. It is extremely important when selecting a school that you find one that offers the program and degree that will satisfy your educational plans. For instance, you would not want to apply to a two-year community college if you already have your bachelor's degree in your own country. You would want to select a university that has a graduate program in your field of study.

One of the unique aspects of education in the United States is that there is very little direct regulation by the federal (national) government. Education for the most part has been left to state and local governments and private enterprises. Most institutions can be initially identified as being public or private based on the way in which they are primarily funded for operation.

There are many ways to get information about the quality of a college or university. There is a process of accreditation that most colleges go through to demonstrate that they meet a standard of "excellence." There is a section below that explains accreditation. Also, many publications rank colleges and universities based on certain criteria that the publications determine are important. The U.S. News and World Report ranks institutions of higher education annually and many institutions feel that this is an important measure. It is extremely important for you to do some research to establish where it is that you want to study and to fully understand the quality and reputation of that institution in relationship to other colleges and universities in the U.S. Not everyone can go to "Ivy League" schools, but there are many choices outside the premiere institutions that can deliver an excellent education with a solid reputation.

Public Colleges and Universities

Public colleges and universities receive a significant amount of their operating budgets from the state governments in which they reside and they must follow similar guidelines as other state-funded, government agencies in their states. In other words, public institutions must serve the needs of all of the taxpayers of the state and they are somewhat limited in how specialized they can be. For example, a public institution could not identify itself as representing a particular religious denomination. This, however, would be perfectly fine for a private institution. The funds allocated (given) by a state to a particular college or university are used to offset the cost of tuition for residents of that particular state. At public institutions you will find an "in-state" tuition rate for residents and an "out-of-state" tuition rate for nonresidents. Most international students who intend to study in the United States on a student or exchange visa will have to pay "out-of-state" tuition rates that can be much higher than "in-state" ones. For example, the undergraduate tuition rates for full-time study at an average-sized public university per academic year (9 months that include Fall and Spring semesters) could be $3,000 for "in-state" tuition and as much as $12,000 for "out-of-state" tuition. There are a few exceptions to this general trend and there are also visas—for instance, diplomatic visas—that often allow students to get "in-state" rates after residency requirements have been met.

Private Colleges and Universities

Private colleges and universities do not receive a large part of their operating budgets from the state. Their funding comes primarily from tuition, alumni (former students) donations, and religious and other private sources. Private colleges generally have the same tuition rates for all students, which can range from $15,000 to $25,000 per year and higher. Many of the most "elite" or "prestigious" colleges and universities in the U.S. are private institutions and they do not fall under the same regulatory restrictions that public schools must follow. Because of this, private institutions have the ability to serve more narrow or specialized student categories if they so choose. For example, there are many colleges and universities that are primarily supported by religious denominations. Also, some private institutions are exclusively for women. Not all private colleges and universities are specialized; some are independent from any particular organization and have a great deal of diversity in their student population.

Whether an institution is public or private may not make much difference to an international student. These institutions also range in size from 600 to 33,000 or more students, and this may be a more important factor. How well would you fit in to a small liberal arts college? Are they prepared to handle the special needs of international students? At a school that has 33,000 students, how much individual support can you expect to get? These are important questions and often this is the area that a good recommendation from an international student who has studied or is studying at the institution can be of help.

STATEMENT OF PURPOSE

You should be very clear about the overall affiliation of a school before selecting it. One way to find out the affiliation of a school is to look in the school's catalogue or on their website for their "mission statement" or "statement of purpose." Please consider the following examples (these descriptions were taken from each school's webpages). Baylor University, a well-known and respected university in Texas that is affiliated with the Baptist church, has a very clear mission statement:

> The mission of Baylor University is to educate men and women for worldwide leadership and service by integrating academic excellence and Christian commitment within a caring community.

The University of Notre Dame, a highly respected school in Indiana, is affiliated with the Catholic church. It describes itself as:

> The University of Notre Dame is a Catholic academic community of higher learning, animated from its origins by the Congregation of Holy Cross.

Brigham Young University, a well-esteemed university in Utah that is affiliated with the Mormon church has as its mission statement:

> The mission of Brigham Young University—founded, supported, and guided by the Church of Jesus Christ of Latter-day Saints—is to assist individuals in their quest for perfection and eternal life. That assistance should provide a period of intensive learning in a stimulating setting where a commitment to excellence is expected and the full realization of human potential is pursued.

Smith College, a prestigious women's college in Massachusetts, has the following statement of purpose:

> Smith College is a distinguished liberal arts college committed to providing the highest quality undergraduate education for women to enable them to develop their intellects and talents and to participate effectively and fully in society.

In contrast, the mission of the University of Maryland, a large public research university, states:

> The University of Maryland, College Park (UMCP), is the flagship institution of the University of Maryland System (UMS). As the comprehensive public research university for the state of Maryland and the original land grant institution in Maryland, UMCP has the responsibility within the UMS for serving as the state's primary center for graduate study and research, advancing knowledge through research, providing high quality undergraduate instruction across a broad spectrum of academic disciplines, and extending service to all regions of the state.

K–12, UNDERGRADUATE, AND GRADUATE EDUCATION

In the United States, education is compulsory (required by law), and children must generally go through twelve years of study from first through twelfth grades. These twelve levels of study are generally broken up into Elementary School, which is first through fifth grades, Middle School, which is sixth to eighth grades, and Secondary School (High School), which is ninth through twelfth grades. An optional preparatory level called Kindergarten falls before first grade. There are variations of how the grades are distributed and there are special programs that combine secondary and college level work. The public school system is often referred to as the K–12 system, which means the kindergarten through twelfth grade system.

Students who graduate from secondary school are prepared to enter the workforce, get specific job training, go to college, or do all of these together. Students who are not able to graduate from secondary school have the option to work and/or get job training. In order to qualify for admission into a college or university, these students must complete an adult or alternative high school program, or take and pass the General Education Diploma (GED) test. The GED can serve as an alternative to a high school diploma. There are exceptions to this rule; many community colleges, as an example, have an "open door" admission policy that allows anyone over eighteen or nineteen to take classes. However, students without a high school diploma or a GED may be limited to nondegree study and will always be at a disadvantage should they decide on further study that is beyond the community college.

Undergraduate education generally refers to the first four years of study at a college or university that leads to a degree. The two most common undergraduate degrees are the two-year associate's degree given by most junior colleges and community colleges, and the four-year bachelor's degree given by colleges and universities. These degrees are divided into different areas based on the nature of their curricula (sets of courses). The most common divisions are Science (A.S. or B.S.), Arts and Letters (A.A. or B.A.), Fine Arts (B.F.A.), and Education (B.Ed.).

The bachelor's degree is normally awarded after completing 120 semes-

---

A useful tip

The first year of study is called the "freshman year," the second is the "sophomore year," the third is the "junior year," and the fourth is the "senior year." Students are officially referred to as freshmen, sophomores, juniors, and seniors based on the number of credits they have completed.

ter credit hours of generally specified coursework. The bachelor's degree has a required number of core or "general education" courses and then upper level courses in a "major" area of study. Students officially identify their program of study by referring to it as their "major." Schools divide their programs and departments based on these majors. For example, a student who plans on going into business might major in Business, Marketing, or Accounting. A student interested in computers might major in Computer Science or Information Systems. Students interested in politics might major in Public Affairs, International Relations, or Political Science. Carefully read the college catalogue from the schools in which you are interested to make sure they have a "major" that covers your area of interest. You will be asked to indicate on your application what your intended major will be. This information will be necessary for the paperwork needed to secure an entry visa. There is often a great variety of individual choice in selecting a major and you have the option to change majors. Be careful though, students who change majors too often waste valuable time and are sometimes unable to graduate in four years. Colleges and universities in the U.S. have academic counselors and advisors available to work individually with students on their academic plans. You may or may not be familiar with the role and function of academic counseling, but you should take full advantage of this service.

Academic counselors are at the institution for the sole purpose of helping students to plan and to understand the complicated process of completing a degree. You should become familiar with the office before registering for your first class, and visit the office regularly until you graduate. Understand that there is a difference between "personal" counseling and academic counseling. Most colleges and universities have offices for both functions, but all accredited institutions have at least an office that is responsible for academic counseling.

After completing an undergraduate program, many people enter the workforce if their undergraduate degree satisfies their needs. However, some people continue studying in graduate or professional programs after completing their bachelor's degree. Several bachelor's degree programs serve as preparation for a professional program, e.g., law school or medical school. Also, some bachelor's degree programs do not give enough instruction in a specific area to prepare a student to work productively in that field and so more focused study is given at the graduate level. Because of tough competition in the job market, a graduate degree can often influence a hiring or promotion decision.

There are many different kinds of graduate degrees. For example, the master's degree is generally 30 to 36 semester credits of focused study beyond the bachelor's degree, and usually a final thesis (research) paper. The doctorate level is generally 60 to 65 credits beyond the master's degree and requires a dissertation (research) paper that represents an original contribution to the field of study. Professional degrees are the Juris Doctorate (J.D.) for lawyers and the Doctor of Medicine (M.D.) degree. These two degrees involve three to five years of study beyond the bachelor's and a residency period.

THE ACADEMIC CALENDAR

No specific calendar is required by law for colleges or universities in the United States. For the most part, colleges and universities follow the same general calendar, with slight variations. The majority of institutions of higher education follow a semester system, although there are a few, particularly "community" or "technical" schools, that follow a quarter system. The quarter system divides the year into four "quarters" that often cover 10 weeks.

A semester system generally consists of two main semesters of 16 weeks called Fall and Spring semesters, with an optional summer term that often ranges from 8 to 12 weeks. The Fall term is generally the term when new students are admitted to the institution, and usually begins at the end of August or early September and runs until mid-December. The Spring term generally runs from mid-to-late January through May. The Summer term often runs from early June to mid-August. International students studying on F-1 or J-1 visas are generally required to be full-time students during the Fall and Spring terms. Summers may be optional, depending on when you are entering the institution. Make sure that you are fully aware of your enrollment responsibilities. This must come directly from your Foreign Student Advisor.

ACCREDITED OR NONACCREDITED SCHOOLS

No government agency directly oversees the quality of postsecondary education in the United States. This is one reason why you must be certain that the school you select is a credible institution. It should meet or exceed a minimum set of standards, and that is confirmed through a voluntary process of accreditation by a regional or national accrediting body. Regional accreditation covers all aspects of a college or university. The prevailing professional association of a field generally does national accreditation, and they generally accredit programs within a university.

There are five regional accrediting bodies: the Southern Association of Colleges and Schools, the New England Association of Schools and Colleges, the Middle States Association of Colleges and Secondary Schools, the North Central Association of Colleges and Secondary Schools, and the Western Association of Schools and Colleges. These regional accrediting bodies are registered with the national Department of Education and they accredit both public and private institutions.

There are numerous national accreditation bodies that accredit professional programs. For example, the American Bar Association (ABA) accredits law schools. All states have regulations that require graduation from an "accredited" law school in order to receive a license to practice law in that particular state. This type of regulation extends to many fields, particularly those that involve the well-being of individuals. Medical schools and dental schools are other examples.

LIBERAL ARTS, RESEARCH, AND LAND GRANT SCHOOLS

Many colleges and universities have a historical character that they try to maintain. This is often reflected in their curriculum (set of courses) and in their missions. Some schools identify themselves as liberal arts institutions or as having a liberal tradition. What they mean is that their curriculum will be very focused in the Humanities. The purpose of the institution is to cultivate minds and to create a well-rounded citizen who can contribute to the culture and preserve traditional democratic values. Research universities are heavy in the math, science, and technical areas and stress the importance of developing the knowledge base. A research university will have departments that are found in liberal arts institutions, but the major resources generally go to the math, science, and engineering areas.

In your search for a school you may run into the term "land grant institution." Land grant colleges and universities have their own unique beginning. They were initially founded on the basis of two initiatives from the federal government, one in 1862 and one in 1890, whereby the government gave each state a grant of land to be used to start colleges and universities. These institutions were formed to serve the rural population and special populations not being well served by existing schools. Most of these schools had an agricultural and technical curriculum. Many land grant institutions have grown to become fine schools and remain strong in the research tradition.

POSTSECONDARY INSTITUTIONS: BASIC DISTINCTIONS*

Junior Colleges

Junior colleges offer general education courses that lead to associate degrees (two-year) in the arts (A.A.) or sciences (A.S.). These are either public or private institutions that usually serve to move students through transfer into a bachelor's degree program at a college or university. They normally have agreements with other colleges or universities that make admission there easier for junior college graduates. Even though the faculty may be required to conduct research, teaching is the primary function of junior colleges. Some of them have on-campus housing, although most do not.

Vocational/Technical Institutes

Training is the main function of these institutions. They offer a variety of programs in specific-skill areas that prepare students specifically for employment. The programs vary in length, but are generally less than two years. They can be public or private, and many of these institutions are proprietary, or used to make a profit like a business. Some of these programs, particularly the public institutes, offer an associate's degree; however, most mainly offer certificates that enable students to show their qualifications to enter a trade. The programs are generally in occupational and technical areas not served by other postsecondary institutions or professional schools. Examples of these include schools that provide training in electronics, hair styling, English-as-a-Second Language (ESL), truck driving, office skills, computer training in software or hardware, and cooking. The list of these kinds of schools is much longer than we have provided here. These institutes normally do not have on-campus housing.

Comprehensive Community Colleges

These are mainly public institutions that offer courses that lead to an associate's degree (a two-year degree), general education for transfer to a college or university, and vocational/technical coursework. Community colleges generally have agreements with other colleges and

---

*Based on Carnegie Classification of Institutions of Higher Educations, Carnegie Commission on Higher Education.

universities that make transferring easier. Teaching and training, not research, are the primary focuses of these institutions. Community colleges normally do not have on-campus housing.

Four-Year Colleges

These colleges mainly offer coursework leading to a bachelor's degree in the arts (B.A.) or sciences (B.S.), which normally takes four years of full-time study to acquire. A four-year college may offer a two-year associate's degree (A.S., A.A.) in a few subject areas; however, they emphasize the bachelor's degree. Teaching is the primary function of these institutions, though the faculty may be required to have their own research agendas. Many four-year colleges have on-campus housing; however, some may not.

Comprehensive College/Upper Level Colleges

These are public or private institutions that offer all that a four-year college does, as well as graduate and/or professional programs. These schools may offer one or two programs at the doctorate level. Teaching is the primary function of these institutions, although the faculty members are often required to have their own research agendas. Many, but not all of these colleges, have on-campus housing.

Universities

These are public or private institutions that offer all that a comprehensive college or upper level college does plus a variety of doctoral programs. Research is important to a university and faculty member, and many of these institutions are primarily focused on their research agendas. Most universities have on-campus housing.

RESEARCH UNIVERSITIES. A research university is a university with research focus. Scientific research is fundamental to the mission of the university and to the faculty. Most research universities have on-campus housing.

FLAGSHIP UNIVERSITIES. Each of the fifty states in the United States has the option to designate one university as its leading school. In doing so, each state invests more money in that institution than in any other institution in the state, which should improve the quality of that particular institution. This does not ensure though that the flagship university is the best university in the state, as there are many private schools. All flagship universities should have student housing.

ELITE UNIVERSITIES. Elite universities are generally private institutions that are highly selective and have large endowments (monetary donations). These institutions vary greatly in the size of their student bodies, but consistently charge over $20,000 per year for tuition. Some examples of elite universities are: **Columbia University** in New York, **Harvard University** in Massachusetts, **Brown University** in Rhode Island, **Yale University** in Connecticut, **Princeton University** in New Jersey, **Dartmouth College** in New Hampshire, the **University of Pennsylvania** in Pennsylvania, Massachusetts Institute of Technology, **Cornell University** in New York, and Stanford University in California. The schools in bold print are known as "Ivy League" schools and they have a long history of competing against each other in sports and other activities.

This is in no way a fully representative list of all the "elite," "prestigious," or even the best colleges and universities in the U.S. You can visit the *U.S. News & World Report* website to see several lists of how they rank colleges and universities at

www.usnews.com/usnews/edu/college/corank.htm

Professional Schools

These schools are either part of a university or separate from a university that prepares students for a specific professional level of employment. A national accreditation body generally accredits these schools, and completion of the program allows the student to practice in that field. Law schools, medical schools, schools of psychology, and dental schools are examples of professional schools.

THE APPLICATION PROCESS AND PACKAGE

Once you have decided on the college or university that is right for your goals, you should contact the school and request application information. Many of them have made this process easier by giving access to materials via the WWW; however, requesting an application package by regular mail establishes a more personal correspondence. Many students are surprised by the early application deadlines given for international students, so we advise you to begin this process at least a year and six months to two years before you intend to arrive in the U.S. to study. Deadlines for completed applications will be given in the application materials that you request, but by the time you receive the documents, the deadline for the term in which you are interested may have passed. Most college guides and websites have application deadlines, so it is very important that you find this information as soon as possible. For example, it is not uncommon for the target date for international student applications to be from early January to early March for the Fall semester, which usually begins late August or early September. Deadlines for Spring admission, are often late July or early August for the term beginning sometime in January. Be aware that some schools only admit international students to begin in the Fall term.

The application package that you will receive can be overwhelming. For some people, the application process can seem so difficult that they "drop out" right away. It is important that you take an organized approach to completing the application. Be patient and only then you can finish the paperwork required by the school. Be sure that you have satisfied all of the items that the school has requested to be sent with the application. Many colleges and universities take a great deal of pride and are often measured against each other by how "selective" they are. This means that many schools receive more applications than they can accept, and they can be very particular about whom they choose to be a part of their academic community. Unlike many other countries, American colleges and universities do not have entrance exams. They try to choose the students who have the best grades, have participated in extracurricular activities, and have shown leadership during their secondary school years. Some examples of extracurricular activities are: participation on the debate team, playing on a sports team, being a cheerleader, participating in a student organization, holding an office in your school's student government, and some other activities. This is a very short list, but it is important for you to present yourself on the application in the best light. Don't let an incomplete or poorly done application prevent you from being admitted to the school that you have chosen!

There is no standard application package for all of the schools in the United States. Each institution sets up its own procedures and these also vary as to whether you are applying as an undergraduate or a graduate student. Most schools ask for a *formal application* to be filled out, an *application fee*, some kind of *transcript* or an official record of your previous educational experience, a *formal essay* detailing your goals and achievements, *recommendation letters*, and *standardized test scores*.

Application

Applications can be requested in writing, via email, and by downloading from the college's or university's website. Also, it may be possible to complete the application directly online from the institutional website. The application is generally used to collect information about the student. You can be requested to write about yourself, as well as provide your educational background, statistical information, study plans, and standardized test scores, which must be supported by official records that have been sent directly from each testing service. Most applications require a signature from the student that holds the student accountable for the information given in the application.

Application Fees

Fees vary from nothing or very little to over a hundred dollars. The average fee is around $35.00. This serves not only as a payment to off-set the cost of processing applications, but to limit applications to those who have serious intentions. Applying to many schools at once can become very expensive.

Transcripts

For undergraduates, a formal scholastic record from secondary school is required. This should indicate your grades, what the grades mean, your final grade point average (GPA), and your date of graduation. If the document cannot be provided in English, then an official translation with the original attached should be acceptable. Your application package should indicate the details.

For graduate students, your undergraduate transcripts need to be officially translated and certified by a university or government official. Most programs will also require that you have your transcripts officially reviewed by a professional evaluation service in the United States. The school you are applying to will indicate what they expect in terms of transcripts; however, it is recommended that you have your transcripts evaluated. Appendix 2 contains a sample list of evaluation services that you might use.

If you have completed some coursework at a university in your country, but have not graduated, it is a good idea to have your transcripts translated and evaluated. You may be able to receive some undergraduate credit for the work that you have done that could save you valuable time and money.

The Essay

The essay should be used to shine light on aspects or highlights about you that were not addressed in the overall application. The application usually gives some guidelines about what is expected in the essay, but please take advantage of the opportunity to show who you really are and where you are going in your future.

Recommendations

Most applications, particularly graduate applications, ask for recommendations (letters of support) from your former professors and other professionals who can evaluate your achievements in academics, extracurricular activities, and community service.

Tests

Most colleges will ask for several standardized test scores. The scores they ask for will differ depending upon whether you are applying for graduate or undergraduate study and upon the kind of program you plan to enter. The following is a list of the most common tests.

TEST OF ENGLISH AS A FOREIGN LANGUAGE (TOEFL). Most international students must submit an up-to-date TOEFL score that meets the college's published requirement. (Exceptions are normally made for students from some English-speaking countries like the United Kingdom, Canada, Australia, and New Zealand.) The scores can range from 500 to 575 for undergraduate programs, and graduate programs often ask for higher scores. There is a new, computerized version of the test that is being implemented that has scores that range from 0–300. For specific information about the TOEFL, visit their website at http://www.toefl.org. The TOEFL is designed to give an indication of whether a student's English language ability is appropriate for suc-

A useful tip

Admission to an ESL program does not mean that the student has been accepted into that institution's academic programs. ESL students generally have to go through the same competitive application process as other students. Some students are surprised when they are not admitted to a university after completing very expensive ESL programs. However, most schools that do issue I-20's for ESL have a very clearly articulated path for students to enter their academic programs and to process a "Level Change" I-20 with the INS.

cessful academic study. Many schools retest students with their own test when students arrive, and some students are placed into ESL courses to complete their language preparation and to support their initial academic study. Some schools will admit students without a TOEFL score directly into their English-as-a-Second-Language (ESL) programs.

SCHOLASTIC ASSESSMENT TEST (SAT)/AMERICAN COLLEGE TESTING ASSESSMENT (ACT).
The ACT and the SAT are standardized tests that most undergraduate programs require of entering freshman (first year students). They measure math and verbal abilities and have components that can assess knowledge in subject areas.

GRADUATE RECORD EXAMINATION (GRE). The GRE is a standardized test that is used to predict a student's potential for graduate study. It measures verbal, analytical, and quantitative skills.

GRADUATE MANAGEMENT ADMISSIONS TEST (GMAT). The GMAT replaces the GRE for students who are interested in studying in a Business Administration (MBA) or management program.

LAW SCHOOL ADMISSION TEST (LSAT). The LSAT replaces the GRE and GMAT for students interested in studying at a law school.

All in all, be advised that the SAT, ACT, GRE, GMAT, and LSAT were designed for native English speakers and that the complicated language structures can make them extra difficult for non-native English speakers.

Visas, Visas!

You cannot just jump on a plane and begin studying in a degree program in the United States. Getting into the country can be very difficult because of strict laws regulating entry into the United States. You must also apply to the U.S. government for a visa appropriate to the program of study you have chosen. The school to which you are applying will provide you with a list of requirements that will be needed to complete your visa application. Both the admission application and the visa application are generally done at the same time. However, the visa application process is not finalized until the school has accepted you and issued the appropriate documents to make a formal application for a visa at the U.S. Embassy or Consulate in your country.

The following is a list of important documents and terms related to visas:

- **Passport.** This is a document that is issued by your government that identifies you as a national of that country and permits you to travel outside of it. A passport must always be kept valid. If you lose your passport or if it expires while you are outside of your country, then you should go to your embassy and immediately get a replacement. Always keep photocopies of all of your documents related to your passport, visa, and any other official documents.

■ **Travel document.** A person who is not a national of a particular country, but resides in that country can be issued a travel document, usually called a Certificate of Identity that will enable the person to travel.

■ **Visas.** A visa is a stamp placed in the passport that gives you permission to enter a particular country. A visa stamp issued by the U.S. Embassy or Consulate should be viewed like an entrance ticket that can be used over and over until it expires. Many people are confused by what a visa does. In short, it lets you into the country.

■ **Visa status.** When a person arrives at a "port of entry" such as an airport, a border crossing, or a seaport in the United States, they are subject to inspection by an officer from the Immigration Naturalization Service (INS). The INS inspector will carefully examine your passport, your visa, and any supporting documents related to your visa. If everything is in order, the inspector will then confer a valid visa status based on the visa stamp in the passport. The visa status is indicated on a small white card that is called a Form I-94. This form is a very important document because it identifies your status and indicates how long you are allowed to stay in the United States.

Once you are admitted into the U.S. and have a valid I-94, your visa stamp in your passport is no longer important. It only will become significant again if you leave the United States. You will then need a valid visa to reenter the U.S. and you will once again be conferred status at the port of entry by an INS inspector through an I-94 card. Your visa status is valid as long as is indicated on the Form I-94. You can lose your visa status if you are found to have violated the terms of your visa. You will then have to either apply to the INS for a reinstatement of your visa status, or leave the country voluntarily.

Many different kinds of visas permit individuals to request entry to the United States. For information concerning visa categories not listed, or for more details about those that are listed, you should contact the

A useful tip

Although your visa stamp can expire while you are in the U.S., your I-94 card must not expire. If you feel like you are going to exceed the date on your I-94 card you should apply for an extension with the INS. They may or may not grant an extension depending upon the reasons that you give and the terms of your visa. You—not the school or your hosts—are solely responsible for maintaining your visa status.

U.S. Embassy or Consulate in your country. The following represents some of the most common temporary visas:

VISA WAVER PROGRAM (WB OR WT). The visa waver program allows visitors who qualify from 29 countries to enter the U.S. without a visa stamp for a period of 90 days. This period of stay cannot be extended nor can it be changed to another status. The countries include: Andorra, Argentina, Austria, Australia, Belgium, Brunei, Denmark, Finland, France, Germany, Hungary, Iceland, Ireland, Italy, Japan, Liechtenstein, Luxembourg, Monaco, The Netherlands, New Zealand, Norway, Portugal, Singapore, San Marino, Slovenia, Spain, Sweden, Switzerland, the United Kingdom, and Uruguay (this is accurate to August 3, 1999). This program is specifically for tourist purposes, and individuals cannot study or work while in the U.S. on a WT. It would be appropriate for someone to visit different schools and gather information about a school and its application procedures, but the visa application would have to be made by the student in his or her home country. Do not enter the U.S. under this program if you intend to study!

VISITOR'S VISA (B-1/B-2). The B visa category is for people who want to visit the U.S. for a period of six months or less. Through application directly to the local Immigration Naturalization Service (INS), it is possible to extend this status for an additional six months. The B-1 category is for visitors who are in the U.S. based on a business or employment outside of the country. The B-2 category is for tourist purposes. Individuals who enter the U.S. in B visa status are not eligible for employment within the country or for full-time study. Therefore, this visa is not appropriate for students who intend to study in the United States. Once an individual is in the U.S. on a B-2 visa, it is possible but not easy, to change it to a Student or Exchange Visitor visa, unless that individual has previously discussed study plans with the U.S. Consul and has been issued a B-2 visa designated "Prospective Student." A person can be denied admission into the country or given a very short stay if during inspection at the port of entry there is evidence that the individual is attempting to enter on a B visa with the intention of studying. An example of some evidence would be this person's school transcripts and diplomas and other education-related documents.

EXCHANGE VISITOR VISA (J-1). This type may be appropriate for certain students and scholars; particularly those sponsored by agencies, foundations, the U.S. government, or their home governments. The purpose of the visa is for cultural and intellectual exchange. It is granted on the presentation of a Certificate of Eligibility (Form IAP-66) and supporting financial documentation from a sponsoring agency. The accompanying dependents of a J-1 Exchange Visitor (a spouse and a child, for example) enter the U.S. on a J-2 visa that may, in some cases, permit employment with approval of the U.S. Immigration and Naturalization Service. It is important to note that in many cases an Exchange Visitor must leave the U.S. at the conclusion of their program, and may not change their visa status until a two-year home country residence has been completed.

STUDENT VISAS (F-1). The F-1 visa is the appropriate visa for a student to obtain to study full-time in the U.S. To enter the United States, international students will need a passport from their government, a visa from the U.S. Consulate, and a properly endorsed Form I-20 with supporting documents from a school. At the port of entry, a student presents an I-20 with supporting documents, and a passport with a valid F-1 visa to the INS inspector. Upon successful inspection, F-1 visa status is conferred by the inspector stamping the Form I-20 and Form I-94 with an entry date and endorsing both the I-94 with the initials D/S. D/S represents "duration of status," which means that the individual will remain in status as long as he or she holds a valid I-20, is pursuing a full course of study, and has complied with the regulatory terms or rules of the F-1 visa.

To apply for a Student (F-1) or Exchange (J-1) visa, a passport and a Certificate of Eligibility (Form I-20 for F-1 and Form IAP-66 for J-1) are needed along with supporting financial documentation. A Form I-20 or IAP-66 will be issued to a student once he or she is admitted to the college or university and has shown documentation of adequate financial support. A student on an F-1 visa must enroll for at least 12 credits each semester in an undergraduate academic program, 9 hours in a graduate program, or at least 18 contact hours in an intensive ESL program. There are strict regulations concerning students studying on F-1 and J-1 visas, and a student on an F-1 visa should be prepared not to work for the first academic year. As we mentioned earlier, a spouse and/or children accompanying the F-1 student would enter the U.S. on an F-2 visa.

DEPENDENT(S) OF F-1 (F-2). The F-2 visa is granted to the spouse or children of an F-1 visa student. Individuals on F-2 visas are eligible for full- or part-time study in the United States, but are *not required* to study. Children on F-2 visas can access public schools without tuition, and would pay the same fees, if any, as any other family living in the community. Individuals on F-2 visas **are not permitted** to work in the United States. Unauthorized employment would be considered a violation of the F-2 visa status.

F-1 STUDENT AND J-1 EXCHANGE VISA APPLICATION. The school that you decide to attend must have the ability to issue Form I-20s if you are seeking an F-1 visa, and they must be able to issue Form IAP-66 for J-1 visas. These are two different programs and some schools may only be eligible to issue one of the forms. The application package that you receive should have a checklist of the papers you need to have prepared in order to qualify for an I-20 or an IAP-66. Schools are required to estimate the total cost of being a student for an academic year, including tuition, fees, living expenses, books, supplies, and medical insurance. International students must be able to show that there are sufficient funds available for study at that financial level.

■ **Finances.** A school that issues I-20s and IAP-66s should include a list of costs in the application package. It will look like the following sample:

Tuition and mandatory fees: *(two semesters)*	$11,000
Living expenses for 12 months: *(includes room, board, local transportation, and incidental costs)*	$10,000
Books and supplies	$750
Medical insurance	$650
Total	**$22,400**

Before the sample school issues you an I-20 or an IAP-66, you will need to present documentation that shows that you have access to funds through personal, family, or sponsors that can cover $22,400 for the year—the sample school estimate. (Of course, the dollar figure will vary depending on the school and its location.) This can be done through a variety of ways, for example a bank statement showing sufficient funds from your own account. If someone is sponsoring you, they must provide a sworn affidavit of support (an official declaration) that includes a bank statement showing sufficient funds, or a letter from their employer showing a sufficient salary, or tax returns from a business, stock portfolios, or any combination of the above. The school will be very clear with you about what they are looking for and will provide any official documents you will need.

Finally, you have your application completed, your test scores in route, your essay, letters of recommendation, transcripts, the application fee, and the financial documentation the school requested for the correct visa sent off to the school. Then you wait and hope for the best. You might then receive a letter requesting more specific information than you had originally sent. If so, you should respond immediately. Or, you might receive a rejection letter stating that the school is highly competitive and therefore you were not accepted. Or, you might receive a letter of acceptance, which you should keep, that either includes your I-20 or IAP-66, or states that it is on the way. You will need your acceptance letter at the embassy or consulate.

Once you receive your full acceptance package from your school you are almost ready to approach the U.S. Embassy or Consulate to request an F-1 or J-1 visa. You should call ahead of time to find out the appropriate procedures for that particular embassy or consulate. It varies from country to country; however, most require that you come in person for an interview with an official in the visa section. You should bring:

- the $45.00 application fee (the amount may change);
- a completed Form OF156 (blank forms are available at the U.S. Consular offices);
- a photograph 37 × 37 mm showing your full face without head covering;
- an acceptance letter, your Form I-20 or IAP-66;
- any supporting financial documents, which should be less than six months old, and any evidence that shows that you plan to return to your home country.

One of the most common reasons for a visa denial is that the student failed to demonstrate appropriate ties to his or her home country. A residence (apartment, home), other property, a job, or strong family ties in your home country may be such demonstrations. The inspecting officer may ask for more documentation,

> ### A useful tip
>
> When you go to the interview, you should have your study plan ready, know your goals, and know why you want to study abroad.

deny your visa, or grant a visa immediately following your interview. If the embassy official asks for more documentation, you should comply as quickly as possible. If your visa application is denied, the inspecting official should tell you why your application is being denied. You should inform your advisor at the school to see if they can help to determine if anything can be done to address the denial. In most cases there is not much that can be done other than to try again at a later date.

After your visa is granted, there is a lot to be done before you leave to prepare for your arrival in the United States.

Chapter 2

Newcomer's Checklist

At the end of Chapter 1, you were leaving the U.S. Embassy or Consulate with a new visa in your passport. To this point you have been accepted into the school of your choice, verified your acceptance, received the appropriate forms from the school and your sponsors, and have success-fully secured a visa to request entry into the United States. What should you do next?

Now, are you ready to fly? Have you sent your travel itinerary to the Foreign Student Advisor of your school? Many schools will provide transportation from the airport if they know when you are arriving. If your school does not provide this service, do you know where you need to go when you arrive and how you are going to get there? Try to make these arrangements in advance, if possible. If not, check on the airport shuttle services. They are often less expensive than a taxi, especially if you are trav-eling very far from the airport. Make sure that you bring all the visa paperwork and your passport on the plane with you. Keep them on your person. Do not leave them in your checked baggage. This will cause an unnecessary delay at the Port of Entry. It is a good idea to arrive at the airport at least two hours early for international flights. There will be some exit processing and baggage checking that can take time.

QUARANTINE

Well in advance of your travels, check with both the U.S. Embassy and the airline with which you are traveling concerning any quarantine, import/export, or immunization requirements pertinent to your exiting your country and entering the United States.

INSPECTION

When you arrive at the airport in the United States you will be at a Port of Entry, and you must go through inspection of your visa paperwork by the Immigration and Naturalization Service and request entry into the United States. If your paperwork is in order, then you are given the appropriate F-1 or J-1 visa status. Your passport and your I-20 or IAP-66 are stamped with an entry date and you are issued a Form I-94 that is stamped with an entry date. For F-1 visa holders, your I-94 and I-20 will be marked with the letters D/S, which represents Duration of Status. D/S means that you are allowed to stay as long as you are maintaining your status and are enrolled in a full course of study. For J-1 visa holders D/S is normally indicated on the I-94 and IAP-66, but it is also possible that a date is entered based on the program completion date. You must initially attend the school that is indicated on your stamped I-20 or IAP-66. If you attend another institution then you have violated your visa and you are out-of-status (see *Maintaining Your Visa Status*, on p. 30.). It is possible to transfer schools after attending for one complete term, but be careful to follow the appropriate procedures.

Following inspection you get your baggage and pass through customs. This is where you must declare any taxable property you are carrying, and your baggage may be inspected for any substances that are not allowed to be brought into the United States, like food or food products or illegal drugs, for example.

After passing through customs, you enter the airport terminal and meet your ride or proceed to the public transportation you have planned to take. Be wary (careful) of any strangers at the airport, particularly anyone who offers you help without you asking them. You should proceed to your temporary or permanent housing from the airport in order to safely store your luggage and to rest from your travels. International flights can take a great deal of energy out of you.

REQUIREMENTS RELATED TO THE SCHOOL

Dates

The first thing that should be done is to check the dates that the school indicates are important. A reporting date is indicated on your I-20 or IAP-66; you must report to the Foreign Student Advisor before that date. This is generally much earlier than the first day of classes. Most schools will have an orientation for incoming international students and you should plan to be there for instruction. Also you need to know the date when you can enter your dormitory or housing arrangement. If you arrive too early you must arrange for temporary housing. Knowing these dates will help you in deciding your arrival date. Buy your airplane ticket early because if you wait too long, it may be more difficult to fly on the date of your choice.

Reporting

You should report to the Foreign Student Advisor (FSA) as soon as possible after arriving in the United States. The FSA works for the school, not for the INS or State Department. FSAs are responsible for advising students concerning the laws and regulations of their visa and to insure that the school follows the regulations related to the privilege of issuing Forms I-20 and IAP-66. Any questions that you may have concerning your visa or visa status should be directed to the FSA.

Bring your passport, Form I-94, and stamped I-20 or IAP-66 with you. Your FSA will make photocopies of these documents and should be a rich source of information. Consider your FSA to be an important contact and be sure to ask him or her questions about things that you may not understand. If the FSA cannot answer your questions, then you will be directed to the appropriate office at your school. Your FSA should let you know what you need to do next. The FSA will inform you of the orientation meetings you should attend and of any registration deadlines. Make certain that you take the required placement test, usually for math and English, as these will determine your ability to register for classes. Your FSA may refer you to any placement tests you need to take prior to registration. He or she will also direct you to your assigned academic advisor or to an academic counselor concerning educational matters.

Academic Advisor/Academic Counseling

Most students are required to meet with an academic advisor who is usually a faculty member in your major, or an academic counselor who is a professional trained in advising students. Given the wide range of choices available to students, academic advising and counseling is very helpful to guide students along the long road to graduation. Colleges and universities in many countries do not provide this service because the curriculum is generally set: every student is given a particular schedule of classes that he or she should take. In the United States, more responsibility is placed on the student for making choices concerning their classes and degrees. Make a plan with your advisor. Remember, there are many interesting classes that are offered at your school. However, do not waste time taking too many classes that are not related to the degree that you are seeking.

Also, try to familiarize yourself with the schedule of classes and the basic requirements of your major. You should be able to work out the classes that you plan to take during the meeting with your advisor. Be sure to have the advisor sign off on your choices so that you can register. Students studying on F-1 and J-1 visas are required to register for a full-time load. This is generally 12 or more undergraduate credit hours, 9 or more graduate hours, or 18 or more contact hours in an Intensive English Program (IEP).

> ### A useful tip
>
> It is your responsibility to register for a full-time load. If you fail to register for a full-time load, then your visa will become out-of-status. Do not blame anyone but yourself if you fail to do that. It is a good idea to check with your FSA after you have registered to confirm appropriate registration.

Housing

Your acceptance package should include an application for housing with a request for a deposit that can be several hundred dollars. Take care of this as early as possible. If the school does not offer housing, then you should arrive early enough to comfortably secure a place to live. Off-campus housing can be unpredictable and expensive. Make sure you give yourself enough time to make a careful selection. Rents for a one-room apartment (often called a single or an efficiency) can range from $400.00 per month in rural areas to over $1500.00 per month in a large city. A security deposit and the first and last month's rent are often required, and most rentals require the signing of a lease, which is a contract to stay for a specific period (normally for one year). Be careful and get help, if possible.

Insurance

Health insurance allows you to get professional medical help according to particular rules and conditions that your insurance plan contains. Health insurance is required for international students at most schools. Many schools require you to use the school's policy or one that meets or exceeds the coverage (available services) of the school's policy. Your school will inform you of any immunizations that you will need and of the ways in which you can cer-

> *A useful tip*
>
> Medical insurance is something that you absolutely must have. Medical costs in the United States can be very expensive, even for what may seem to be a minor visit. If the school does not require that you get medical insurance, get it anyway!

tify them. It may be more comfortable for you to get these shots before coming to the U.S. from your own doctor, but if you do, make sure you get the appropriate documentation. There may be immunization requirements prior to entering the United States. These requirements differ from country to country, so you are well advised to check with the U.S. Embassy or Consulate in your home country for details.

Many students have found out the hard way how expensive healthcare can be in the U.S. and have had to interrupt or even end their studies because a large medical bill had exhausted their funds. Do not mess around with insurance issues. Get your medical insurance and do not get caught in a bad situation without it.

Registration for Classes

Registration involves more than just selecting your classes with an advisor or an academic counselor. There is the physical process of submitting your registration and paying your tuition. For some colleges this is done via a specific office or by mail. For many schools this can now be done via the telephone or the World Wide Web. After you have submitted your schedule request, you may receive written confirmation and a bill. Learn more about registration and payment procedures in your college or university. Some schools expect you to pay immediately after registering. Check with your FSA or a counselor for the correct procedures.

A NOTE ABOUT ESL. Usually, your TOEFL score accurately represents your ability to use the English language. Most students, however, are surprised by their "low" placement after taking an ESL placement test. The students often feel that they could have done better if they had had more time for the test. In addition, students often have an inflated (exaggerated) sense of their English proficiency. Time indeed is an important factor of most placement tests and quite often we make wrong judgments about our own ability to communicate in a foreign language. Do not be upset if you are placed at a lower level than you expected. If you are really placed in the wrong level, the teacher will notice and most programs have a way to move students in the first week. However, you should not expect to be moved up a level just because you want to move. If you are placed in a level that is too high, you will not learn as much and you will become a burden on the students that belong in the class. ESL programs maintain their quality by being careful to accurately place students in the appropriate levels and by moving them efficiently and effectively through the levels.

It is extremely important that you have the appropriate English language skills to handle college level instruction. Having to struggle with the language and the content of a course at the same time can put a student far behind the rest of the class. If you have a problem with English, get help either through an ESL program, the academic counseling center, the college tutoring center, or the college reading and writing center. Any of these offices should be able to direct you to a source of help. Also, many community or adult education programs offer ESL classes that may help.

MAINTAINING YOUR VISA STATUS

As indicated in Chapter 1, there is a distinction between a visa and visa status. The Department of State issues visas at the U.S. Embassy or Consulate in your country. A visa allows you to enter the U.S. to request admittance from the INS at the Port of Entry. The INS confers a visa status upon inspection. You should be very clear concerning the regulations related to your visa. These vary between F-1 and J-1 visas. Basically, you can maintain your status by always registering for a full-time load of classes, by attending classes and doing the work required by the professor, by making sure that your paperwork is kept up-to-date, by not working without INS approval (you can get on-campus employment for 20 hours or less per week). This is a very simplified list. To obtain a more detailed list, meet with your FSA. If you are determined to be out-of-status by your FSA, then you must either return home or go through a complicated paperwork process that involves making a formal request to the INS for a reinstatement of your visa status. This process requires a detailed explanation of why you were unable to meet the requirements of your visa. Do not expect that you will automatically be granted a reinstatement. You must convince the INS that there was a just cause for your falling out-of-status. This application currently costs $120.00 to process.

EMPLOYMENT

Employment regulations for J-1 visa holders are based on the terms of the program. J-1 students should meet with their FSA to be clear as to what those terms are. F-1 students are not eligible for off-campus employment during their first academic year (9 months, Fall and Spring semesters). Regulations allow for work on-campus; however, F-1 students should meet with their FSA to determine employment eligibility and authorization procedures prior to accepting any employment. After a student has completed one academic year of study, there are possibilities for other forms of employment off campus. You should discuss the possibility of off-campus employment with your FSA and under no circumstances should you accept any job without careful and direct consultation with your FSA.

SOCIAL SECURITY NUMBER/ TAX IDENTIFICATION NUMBER

This is usually a very confusing area for international students. From the Social Security Administration's (SSA) point of view, a social security number (SSN) is used for employment purposes only and is not a national identity number. An SSN is not required for securing a bank account or getting a driver's license. In reality, unfortunately, not having an SSN can make life difficult for an international student because many institutions in the United States do not interpret the SSA's explanation about a social security number correctly. According to regulations, only those F-1 and J-1 students who are authorized for employment and have a job offer can receive an SSN. Students who are not authorized for work should receive a Tax Identification Number (TIN). All students on F-1 and J-1 visas must file a tax return by using the IRS Form 1040NR, whether you have worked or not. See your FSA concerning general filing requirements. The TIN functions in much the same way as an SSN and can be used in place of an SSN. Examples are that when you apply for a lease on an apartment, to get a credit card, or to buy a car, you may be asked for an SSN. The TIN should satisfy any of these requests.

AMERICAN LAW

One thing that strikes international students once they have arrived is that—although the United States is known as "the land of the free"—there seems to be a lot of rules to follow and many signs that go with those rules! During a seminar, one student exclaimed, "Everywhere I turn I either see the word *no* or *don't* attached to a rule!" Well, the student is correct. The United States does give its citizens a great deal of political freedom, but along with that goes personal responsibility. On a day-to-day basis, people in this country are more conservative than they would like to admit. There are many laws that govern social behavior that you must become aware of before you unknowingly break the law. "I did not know about this law," some students say. Unknowingly breaking the law is not an excuse that will hold up in a court of law. The easiest laws to break for any student have to do with two major responsibilities: drinking alcoholic beverages and owning and operating a car.

College life does not take place exclusively in the classroom. College is a time when many students experience life for the first time outside the direct control of their parents. This newly found freedom is for some students an opportunity to come into their own and show how they can responsibly manage their lives. For

A case to think about

Albert had a difficult but successful day on campus. He registered for the classes, paid tuition and fees, and had a whole evening ahead of him free. He stopped by a 7-11 store and bought a bottle of beer. The weather outside was hot and humid and he decided to sit down near the store and drink his beer. He found a place on a curb of the road—happy and relaxed—and opened the bottle. In a few minutes he noticed a police car pulled over near the place he was sitting and a cop approaching him. "Do you know what you are doing now?" asked an officer. "Yes, I am drinking beer," replied Albert smiling. "Is anything wrong with it? It is just a beer . . ."

Yes, there was something wrong in Albert's case. In the state where it happened, drinking alcohol from opened bottles in public places is considered an offense. Because of this seemingly "minor" episode, Albert's future as a student is now in serious jeopardy.

others, it is an opportunity to test their personal limits, and this often, unfortunately, ends up in some kind of problem for the student. The problems can range from an inability to keep up with the work required in class, to direct conflict with the police. The role of alcohol and drugs on college campuses is an area of hot news and debate, and one cannot view a college or a university as a sanctuary from the rules that govern a civil society. Be careful! International students are no different than any other students before the law.

It is important to take time to understand your new environment and your role in it. The college, the community surrounding the college, or the law, simply does not tolerate certain types of behavior. Consider drinking, for example. There are very severe penalties for driving while intoxicated (DWI) that can affect your stay in the U.S. and the rest of your life. You should be careful even if you are not driving a car, as there are strict laws that regulate over-consumption and underage drinking. Most states set

A story . . .

This is a story that was told to the authors by a faculty member at a large institution. One day while I was grading papers, I looked out my window (I have a great view) and saw a police officer pulling over a very nice sports car. This was happening right in front of my window! The car was sleek and flashy and looked like it could go very fast. The police officer got out of his car and he seemed to be quite upset. The driver of the car was smiling as if he didn't care much about what was going on. His smile vanished as the police officer invited him outside and placed him in handcuffs. The driver was then taken away by another officer. The arresting officer then removed the license tags from the vehicle, searched it completely, and had it towed. There was clearly a big difference between what the driver of the car thought was going to happen to him and what the police officer did.

the legal age to drink alcoholic beverages at 21 years old. Any violation of these laws may cause serious consequences, including deportation from the country.

There will be many opportunities to enjoy college life. There is always something to do and much of it does not involve drinking alcoholic beverages. It will be very easy to avoid the problems surrounding alcohol abuse on campus by making wise choices. Much of this involves with whom you choose to associate. Choose your friends wisely and have fun. For many, the friends you make in college will be your friends for life! Don't mess it up by challenging the law or rules, and even worse, getting hurt or hurting someone else.

BUYING A CAR

Having a car can be expensive and is a serious responsibility. Owning a car in the United States involves a surprising number of steps. For most people, buying a car is not a pleasant experience. It is often a difficult and confusing process. Most of us do not know much about cars, even if we drive one every day, so it is hard to be sure when you are getting a good deal on a car, and we all want to get a good deal, right? New car prices are normally not fixed and often are deliberately inflated (raised) in order to allow for some haggling (negotiation of the price). Many Americans will tell you that they have "been taken" or deceived when they were buying a car. These feelings are the result of the vagueness related to buying a car.

Do a great deal of research before buying a new car. If you are buying a new car, visit as many different dealerships as possible to compare prices. Also, find out what other people have paid for their cars and ask them for advice or help. Make sure that you are very clear about all of the charges the dealership attempts to impose and question any that seem to be too high or unnecessary. Car dealerships and car buying services that have fixed prices are becoming more and more popular. You may want to find out which particular auto makers offer fixed pricing and compare their prices to other dealerships. Also, there are leasing options that do not require purchasing the car: you use a car for two or three years and then return it back to the dealer. Be very careful of hidden costs in leases that are connected to mileage. In all cases make sure that you understand all of the details involved in your purchase or lease and be sure to read the "fine print." The fine print is generally where details that may be unattractive to the buyer are hidden. Also, getting a loan to pay for a new car may be difficult. You should try to go to your own bank (in the United States) to get a low interest loan, but do not be surprised or offended if they do not give you a loan. You may not have been in the country long enough to have established a credit history, which banks rely on to make loan decisions. You may have better luck at the dealership, but do not get caught up in a high interest loan.

Buying a used car is often a good option. However, if you find a used car that you are seriously considering buying, take it to an auto mechanic and have it thoroughly checked out. It is worth the extra money to have an expert assess the car. You do not want to buy someone else's problem or a car that has been wrecked and repaired for a quick sale. A good used car can save the depreciation (immediate reduction of value) of buying a new car and can be reliable transportation. Make sure that you receive a receipt and the Certificate of Title for the vehicle and that the previous owner properly signs over the title to you.

When you purchase a car, you must get the car licensed for the state in which you reside. To do this you normally have to pay a tax on the value of the car and a fee. Also, it is normal to be required to get the car officially inspected at the appropriate location. If you buy a new car, most of this is done for you at dealership. If you buy a used car, you have to take care of the legal details yourself. Be very careful to study the legal requirements of the state in which you live that apply to keeping your vehicle legal. Many states require annual (yearly) inspections and emissions testing, and some cities and counties require local stickers that have fees attached. With a purchase of a car you must then get automobile insurance. This is required in most states; however, if you purchase a car from a dealer, it may be only expected that you will get insurance. Many students do not consider this in their planning, however, automobile insurance can be very expensive. For a new car, the monthly insurance payment can be as much as the car-payment for a car loan: from $100 to $200 per month and even higher. Nevertheless, you must get auto insurance; this is not an option. The consequences of not having auto insurance in an accident can ruin your life and the other people's lives that may be involved in that accident.

GETTING A DRIVER'S LICENSE

If you are going to drive in the U.S. you will need to get a driver's license from the state in which you reside, even if you have an international driver's license. Driving in the United States is a very important responsibility and you can easily get into trouble if you do not completely understand the traffic laws. You must have your driver's license, your vehicle registration, and proof of insurance in your vehicle at all times when you are driving. In order to get a driver's license you should call the nearest official state office and find out what is required to secure a license. Generally, you will be required to take a written test, a driving test, and have your vision (ability to see) tested. You should bring your passport, your I-20 or IAP-66, and a letter that verifies that you are a student from your school. You will have to pay a fee, as well.

BANKING IN THE UNITED STATES

You should establish your own bank account as soon as possible after arriving. You do not need an SSN or a TIN to establish a bank account, but you should bring your passport, your I-20 or IAP-66, and a letter from the school verifying admission. If a bank insists on an SSN, then go to another bank. If you cannot find a bank that will start an account for you, then go to the local Social Security office and report your experience. They should give a letter for you to bring to the bank explaining the current law. Many colleges and universities have a bank on campus and that bank should take care of your needs. If there are any persistent problems, then report your experience to the FSA and he or she can contact the bank on your behalf.

Many types of accounts are available. The most common are **checking** and **savings** accounts, or a combined version of these. Checking accounts are used to keep the day-to-day cash that you need. They generally carry little or no interest, which is a percentage of money you receive back based on how much you keep in the bank. Savings accounts carry a higher percentage of interest, but you have less access to these accounts. Combined accounts are interest-bearing checking accounts that generally carry more interest than checking accounts, but less than a savings account. Some types of accounts offer higher interest rates than savings accounts, but they often carry early withdrawal penalties or risk if they are based on investments in the stock market. Be careful to understand the terms of your accounts. The bank may charge fees for not maintaining a particular balance in your account or for writing more than a certain number of checks per month. Once again, read the fine print in your bank agreement. Also, there may be charges connected to using automatic teller machines (ATM or money machines), including when you make a purchase using your ATM card at a store.

A useful tip

Do not share a bank account with a friend. We are not suggesting that you should not trust anyone. However, there are too many unpleasant stories to tell about what has happened to other people in such situations. There is absolutely no need to put your money in someone else's account. Get your own.

CREDIT CARDS

The use of credit cards is very popular in the United States. They are a very convenient way to make purchases and monitor your spending, and are often required for securing services like rental cars and hotel rooms. They carry with them the responsibility of using them wisely and not spending beyond your ability to pay. It is a good idea to get a Visa or a MasterCard in your own country before you come to the United States. This is because you will not have a credit history established in the United States when you arrive and you may have trouble getting a card here. Credit cards charge interest on the balance that you keep (the money you owe) and the interest is often very high. Try to keep little or no balance on your cards.

TELEPHONE SERVICE

When you move into your dormitory room, apartment, or house, you might want to establish telephone service. There are a variety of local and long distance service options, including options that give reduced rates for international calls. Be careful about making too many international calls because even with the best rates, it can get very expensive. It is not unusual to hear from some students who love to talk on the phone that their monthly telephone bills are $200 to $300 or even higher. Get as much information about each service option and choose the best one to fit your needs. It is also possible to purchase long distance calling cards that can be used like an ongoing account. Be careful to shop for the best deals.

INTERNET SERVICE AND EMAIL SERVICE

More and more colleges and universities are giving to their students e-mail and on-campus access to the Internet. Colleges and universities value the richness offered by the Internet and they often subscribe to many research databases and online journals. Make sure that you take the time to become aware of the online resources available to you. The school library is generally a good place to begin. Most of the time this does not include Internet service for your home. There are many Internet service providers that cost less than $15.00 a month and as a student it can be a beneficial resource if used properly. It can also keep phone bills down if you can communicate with your family, relatives, and friends back home via email. We will get back to the Internet-related issues again in Chapters 6 and 10.

GETTING READY

You have finally settled into your new living space and have registered, confirmed your registration, and paid for your classes. You are ready to begin and it is probably several days away from the first day of class. There are many issues that you could take care of while you are waiting.

The first thing to do is to become more familiar with the school. Find out as much as you can about the services provided by the college. Find out about recreational facilities, sports programs, social events, clubs, and transportation. Get off campus and find out what the surrounding area has to offer.

Another thing you could do is to buy your textbooks. Do not forget to keep your receipt! Sometimes classes are cancelled, the professor may have changed the books, or you may find the need to change classes. Also, do not write in your books until you are firmly in the class. You may not want to write in your books at all because many schools and bookstores will buy your textbooks back for resale. You will receive a reduced refund for the book, but it often helps. In addition, you may want to cut down on the amount you pay for textbooks by buying those marked "used."

THE FIRST DAY

The first day of classes can be both very interesting and very confusing. It is a challenging day for everyone, so if you experience uncertainty or anxiousness, you are having normal feelings. A word of advice: be on time to class! Punctuality is important for most professors (even if they are sometimes not punctual themselves!).

Patience is important on the first day. You must be prepared for the possibility that what you presumed would be an orderly movement through the day may seem more like chaos. Colleges and universities are like any other large institutions and sometimes small changes have great effects. Classes can get moved from one classroom to another or cancelled; information about such changes is often just a note on the door. If you cannot find a class or if one of your classes is cancelled, you should see your FSA or an academic counselor for help. If a class gets cancelled and brings your load down to less than full-time, you must find a new class to replace it. We have mentioned this already: it is your responsibility to maintain a full-time load of classes.

Your first day of each class will most likely consist of an introductory session and the distribution of the course syllabus (description). The professor might give a clear verbal description of the course and the objectives and present what he or she expects from the students. If a professor does not do this, then the information is usually reflected in the syllabus. Do not expect your class or your professor to be like classes and professors in your own country. They may be very different and the professors may expect things of you that are different from what you anticipate (see Chapter 4 for a detailed analysis).

Chapter 3
Overcoming Culture Shock

It is said that when visiting a town nearby, Nasraddin Hodja—a character in Turkish fairy tales—was stopped by a man who asked what day of the week it was. "I cannot tell you," Nasraddin Hodja replied to the man. "I am a stranger in this town. I do not know what day of the week they have here." This anecdote should perhaps suggest that we sometimes see the differences between America and our home country as greater than they really are. For some people, their personal difficulties, lack of communication skills, and absence of success are easy to explain by differences between cultures. "This country is so different from mine that I cannot be successful here," some may think. Psychologists say that the process of adjustment to a new culture is not an easy process. Your first steps into the new culture are often accompanied by a **culture shock,** an initial reaction of adjustment to a different cultural environment. Culture shock has many different forms and is felt by individuals in a variety of ways. But in most situations it is an unpleasant experience. Let us examine what various people say abut their initial adjustment to the United States. We will later discuss what a student can do to overcome his or her culture shock.

CULTURE SHOCK AS NOSTALGIA

For many of us, culture shock is a reaction of sadness about missing something very dear to our heart. We leave our friends and relatives. We often miss food, familiar smells, colors, and landscapes. Here are just a few examples taken from student interviews: "At the beginning, I missed the food. My childhood was built on that." (J. J., Afghanistan). "I definitely was missing the town, the mountains, and the Caspian Sea." (A. A., Iran). "I missed the smell of my home country, the early morning smell. You have to experience this to understand me." (R. D., India). "Trees, definitely the trees and the aroma of hay. And the snow. I was missing it too." (K. R., Russia). Nostalgia is a bittersweet longing for things and situations of the past, especially those that are impossible to get back to.

For others, their nostalgia is associated with people. "I missed my big family. I felt empty without it. It was a devastating [feeling] during my first year here." (K. O., Bolivia). "I lost the connection. People in my country have closer ties with each other than people here have. I missed open doors that we had at home." (T. T., Russia). "I missed family gatherings, holidays, family prayer, and dancing together. Now I can deal with this. But at the beginning my sadness was huge." (M. K., Ethiopia). "Above everything else, I missed my friends. I clearly remember this feeling of sadness." (R. K., Korea).

Our anxiety and nostalgia are often based on feelings of separation. "I have never been isolated from my family before. That year was my first time alone and it contributed to my painful experiences. I missed my parents, my family. I was blaming America for my misery when, in fact, it was just a discomfort caused by my separation," described a 22-year-old student from Venezuela.

> ### *For class discussion*
>
> Have you experienced these feelings of loss? Do you experience them now? If you can, please share with others about who and what you miss the most from your home country. What do you do about these unpleasant feelings?

CULTURE SHOCK AS LOSS OF PERSONAL CONTROL

When individuals experience culture shock, they may lose some sense of control of the events around them. Simple things such as knowing a weather forecast for tomorrow, getting local news, being able to buy certain food, may bring a sense of comfort. Unfortunately, especially during the first weeks and months of adjustment, these "small" things are missing for many of those who are new to this country. This loss of personal control may create anxiety and frustration. Why does it happen?

Back in our home countries, we used to rely on our friends, important customs, and even unspoken rules that, like a web, connected people together. In most situations, you knew what to say and how to act. America in some ways is different from your home and it takes time to learn the new rules, to make new friends, and to acquire new habits. "Back home, I used to solve all my problems by picking up the phone," an engineer from Turkey recalls of his first college year in America. "When I moved [to the United States], it was especially difficult to accept the fact that my old connections meant nothing here." Before we learn the new rules, our confusion may last quite a long time. "First of all, I didn't have friends," said Mary, a 24-year-old student from South Africa. "I had no idea what people my age were into. I didn't know if the movies or mall were the cool places to hang out. I didn't even know what people of my age were like. I felt like I was being pulled in many different ways. Should I be changed just to meet the American lifestyle? Should I stay where I was? I was confused."

Please do not forget, the more control you have over events around you, the more comfortable you feel, the less noticeable culture shock is.

> ### For class discussion
>
> Did you experience such a loss of personal control over the events around you after your arrival to the United States? If yes, how long did it last? Who did you expect to help you? Who helped you the most during your first month in the United States?

CULTURE SHOCK AS DISSATISFACTION OVER LANGUAGE BARRIERS

For many people, their culture shock is associated with an unpleasant experience of misunderstanding and isolation. Language problems significantly reduce the number of people you are able to contact. Dissatisfaction with the new life therefore can become overwhelming. A 19-year-old Ukrainian student recalls her first day in America: "I was left alone in a foreign country, knowing nobody, speaking no language, having no idea of what was going on. I couldn't read the street signs and I felt myself like on another planet." Isolation may have multiple consequences. The same student continued: "Even being here for about a year, because of my [poor] language, I am still afraid to meet people, the 'real' Americans."

This is how a young woman describes her first year experiences in America after her family moved here from Thailand: "I didn't understand people around me. I hated school and everybody in it. I couldn't wait to go home where I felt safe and secure. Everyone had someone to talk and walk with during lunch. I was always by myself about everywhere I went. I felt so hurt that I cried when no one was around." "Since my English skills were poor, I tended to trust whatever people told me," reported a 29-year-old student from the Philippines. "I tried to convince myself that my skills were not bad, but I kept making so many bad judgments based on my poor language skills. I was not only losing money and comfort, I was losing my self-confidence. I could speak the language well enough to get around but I wasn't proficient. And the saddest thing for me was my inability to understand jokes. That is why many newcomers do not feel very comfortable in America during the first several months because they do not get all those sarcastic and other funny things, especially on TV."

A personal sense of isolation is a major challenge, and there are not many effective ways to fight it alone. Until adequate communication skills are achieved, many people withdraw, whereas others remain frustrated for a long time.

For class discussion

Did you experience difficulties of misunderstanding other people? Have you ever felt embarrassed because of this? Did you feel that sometimes people could not understand you? Did you feel disappointed about having these problems? Did you ever blame yourself for the lack of your language skills?

CULTURE SHOCK AS LOSS OF HABITS AND LIFESTYLE

Culture shock may be reflected by a change of the individual's lifestyle. Like being in a dark room with no lights on, you have to examine every unfamiliar object just to get around: The time you wake up and go to bed, the breakfast you have, the newspapers you read, the people you call, the friends you meet, the food you buy, and the problems you solve. Everything is rearranged like pieces in a jigsaw puzzle. "Suddenly we were told that we would be moving to America," recalls a business major from Peru. "I remember I took a look on our tiny apartment because my dad said that I might never see it again. I didn't believe him, but he was right. Everything changed so suddenly. From being a child and a follower, I have changed and become a serious man. Within a month, I have changed because here in America I didn't have that laid-back atmosphere that we had back home."

Perhaps the most difficult thing about all the rules and customs of the United States is the need to follow these practices and customs. "I hated everything here during my first months. I realized that the rules of behavior here were more strict than those in Argentina," noted a 24-year-old business major. "People obey the rules here. I remember my impressions about traffic in Portland. Cars are standing in lanes and follow each other. In Argentina, you use any and every shortcut to get there faster: any pavement, an opposite side of the road, you run a red light. I know some people do it here but it is uncommon. I may sound like I am a bad person but I am saying how difficult it was to change my habits." A Korean student recalls how she was brought to the United States at age 11 and was moved to a small midwestern rural town. Being "normal" and "regular" in Korea, she suddenly became the center of attention in the town. The family found itself in a spotlight. It was a friendly attitude, very curious and very sympathetic. "We were the only Asian family in town. People would turn around to stare at us. We were different from the local crowd," she told me with a smile. "Did you have cows in Korea? Do people use flush toilets? Do people sing songs in Korea?" These and many other questions of this kind were addressed to her family every day. She reported that the change from being "almost invisible" back in her home country to a local celebrity was overwhelming. The family found itself in a human zoo, not in a cage of course, but on constant display.

> ## For class discussion
>
> Loss of habits or lifestyle is not necessarily an unpleasant experience. One of our students suggested that right after he became a student, he developed many valuable skills that helped him to be independent. Now think about yourself. After your arrival in the United States, did you acquire new habits that you consider useful and valuable? Did you lose some habits that you're glad you got rid of?

CULTURE SHOCK AS PERCEIVED DIFFERENCES

We do not live in vacuums. Our lives are a continuous adjustment to the new. Discovery is usually a pleasant experience. However, there is a difference between discovering something new and accepting it. The authors have seen many cases when a person would experience culture shock because of his or her strong desire to conform to main-stream norms but experience an inability to do so. On the other hand, some individuals are able to protect themselves from culture shock because they do not conform at all but preserve surroundings typical for their home country. They speak only the native language, communicating only with people from the same ethnic group, and try not to travel outside of their neighborhood. However, living in such an isolated environment is impossible for a student. We have to live in a world of values and norms that can be different from those of our cultures.

We are all used to doing certain things in a particular way, like praying, celebrating holidays, following customs, singing, eating, and speaking. We experience difficulties when the current situation

Think critically

Some vivid differences between American culture and other cultures are mentioned frequently in the interviews (1995–2000). *Question:* Do you agree with the observations listed below? Do you think that some people exaggerate the differences between America and their home countries? What can you add to or delete from this list?

- Clothes some people wear in the United States are considered as "strange," "shocking," "revealing" (reported primarily by students who grew up in small towns or rural areas).
- People on the street do not pay attention to you (reported by those who live and study in big metropolitan areas).
- Food is tasteless or not spicy enough (reported generally about fast food).
- Traffic on the roads is overwhelming (reported by those who live in big metropolitan areas).
- Toilets are unusually clean and free of charge (reported by students from both rural areas and from developing countries).
- Television is shocking and revealing (reported mostly by people from "traditional" cultures).
- Telephones and emails are "overused," i.e., everything is solved over the phone or online, there is little personal contact among people (reported by people from "traditional" countries).
- Young people are not cultured and most are not really respectful to adults (reported by most observers).

requires us to follow the majority that does these things differently or doesn't do them at all. Recalls a student from Virginia about his early experiences with America: "Food was a shock to me. Koreans eat Kimchi, a traditional food with garlic and pepper. It gives you a garlic breath. I realized how people here disliked this odor. I stopped eating it after several weeks here and that was very difficult to me because American traditional food was tasteless for me at that time. Another tradition was also difficult to follow. Americans wear shoes in the house, but Koreans never do that. First, I felt extremely embarrassed when people didn't let me take off my shoes when I was visiting their homes, and I felt that others were rude when they did not take off their shoes in my home."

Obviously, similarities between your home culture and American life may substantially reduce culture shock.

CULTURE SHOCK AS PERCEIVED VALUE DIFFERENCES

How often do you feel that your personal values are different from the values of most people around you? How often do you notice that people can freely and carelessly talk about something—like sex or other intimate issues—you consider shameful? How often do you notice that everybody avoids talking about something that you feel is indeed simple and understandable? Many values that may have been accepted in your culture are not understood or even respected in the host country. One of the elements of culture shock is disappointment based on perceived differences of values between two cultures. What values that are widely accepted in the United States are somewhat difficult to accept by those who are going through an adjustment process? Below are some common themes regarding value differences.

American Pragmatism

Such values as material success and achievement are seen not only as typical American traits, but also as a source of disappointment and resentment in many individuals, especially during their initial stage of adjustment. "Pragmatism is shown everywhere. There is little spontaneity in life. Everything is calculated. You have to make an appointment to take somebody for lunch," as a 26-year-old Russian student describes her impressions during the first year. American pragmatism is often seen as instant categorization of everything, as a student from El Salvador almost complained to the authors: "I was really surprised at the beginning with how here in America things should be categorized. Everything should be on its shelf! Sports teams receive ranks. Music groups have ranks. The stock market is all about numbers. Opinion polls are [published] in every newspaper and people also have to be put in racial categories, for example, when they fill out a government form." Disappointment with American pragmatism may also be explained by the fact that most people who try to settle down in the United States are neither rich nor well-to-do individuals. Most newcomers work hard for their daily bread, pay bills, and wonder why so many people around them care about investment, whereas they cannot maintain even a minimal balance in their checking account. Indeed, great numbers of Americans inherited substantial wealth from their parents and ancestors. And millions of individuals born and raised in this country have been able to save more money and establish more connections than millions of those who are still relatively new to this country. Disappointment with materialism causes frustration. This frustration may cause rejection of the existing reality and prolong one's culture shock.

Think critically

Do you agree with the following description of American pragmatism given to us by a student from Spain?

"People here are self-absorbed and stressed. The pressure of life and work in this area seems to take its toll on the quality of life. People have conceivable material comfort and high-tech equipment, and yet many are not happy. People do not even find the time to enjoy a sunset. In comparison, although the pace and pressure of life in Madrid are also intense, it is more a group-oriented, cafe-style society, where social interaction and verbal communications are their 'daily bread'! The American lives to work; in Spain, they work to live."

Do you think that it is possible to interpret American pragmatism from a different, more positive, perspective? Could you suggest, for example, that American people work hard and enjoy working? Could you imply that every nation has its own "style" of work and leisure and Americans are not necessarily unhappy because they have such busy lives?

American Individualism

Individualism is a concern for oneself and one's immediate family as opposed to collectivism, a concern for the larger social groups to which one belongs. In the individualistic culture, people are independent both vertically (people of both higher and lower status levels) and horizontally (people of the same status level). In collectivist cultures, group goals (related to country, community, work, religion, education, and cultural traditions) play the most important role in the individual's life. In individualistic cultures, the goals of the individual and his or her immediate family are the most important ones. Every culture has elements of collectivism and individualism. However, America is viewed by the vast majority of people as a culture with predominantly individualistic features. For many people, especially for those who grew up in collectivist societies, America is seen as a relatively cold, indifferent country filled with selfish individuals.

Such contrasts of experience sharpen our negative evaluations of our present conditions and contribute to culture shock. "People have so many opportunities to do things on their own therefore they do not value friendship," suggested a 19-year-old student from Morocco after spending three years in Ohio. Very often, perceived differences in norms make people see American culture as noncaring. "The families in U.S. are not nearly as close-knit as those in West Africa. There almost everyone just stays with their families for their whole lives. There was open space for children and animals to run and play together. It was my biggest challenge here to get used to empty streets and empty front yards," points out a 24-year-old nurse. "People are superficially friendly here," said a 20-year-old student from Honduras. "It was deceiving at the beginning of my life here and therefore my disappointment was especially strong. People ask questions and do not care about your answers. You ask a person 'how are you' and he will reply 'fine' without even looking at you."

For class discussion

Do you think that American individualism is necessarily a negative characteristic of people and society in general? Do you think that such issues as respect for private property, individual privacy, and civil freedoms can be considered as aspects of American individualism? Please find and discuss examples of the positive impact of individualism on people's lives.

Americans Have "Too Much Freedom"

When one mentions "too much," the question can be asked, "too much compared to what?" It is common for many of us to long for the "good old times" when things seemed to be more certain, the grass greener, the skies bluer, and everything appeared to be in its place. From another standpoint, "too much freedom" would probably mean that today people are granted opportunities and allowed to exercise behaviors that were not considered appropriate some time ago. For newcomers, however, the expression "too much freedom" is associated with their own perceptions of freedom formed in their home countries. Those perceptions, of course, have been shaped according to particular religious principles, ethnic customs, cultural norms, and even political traditions. For a Dutch businessman, American culture could be seen as less free, compared to his home country where, for example, marijuana and prostitution are conditionally legalized. A student from Greece or Russia would notice how much stricter the antismoking rules are in the United

Think critically

Very often, public misperceptions feed people's expectations about America and produce unreasonable expectations and wrong opinions. For example, as we mentioned earlier, there were several highly publicized cases about American children challenging their parents in courts. Americans have expressed a wide range of diversified opinions about these cases with most people disagreeing or feeling outraged by the practices. However, around the world, the cases in which children filed suit against their parents were frequently portrayed as "typically American." It is interesting what one 18-year-old student, born in Pakistan, recalled about his initial perception of America five years ago. "My father had told me that we are moving to a country where children can sue their parents. He wasn't joking. He was serious. I saw his eyes when he explained it to our mother. And they both shook their heads. I was scared first because I felt that everyone would sue me here. I didn't completely understand the meaning of this word, but I knew it was something really bad, when a child can put his parents in jail."

Question: Can you recall any wrong perceptions or expectations you had about the United States prior to your arrival here but later changed your opinions to more positive ones?

States than in their countries. However, for millions of human beings coming to the United States, this country's norms are seen as more "loose" than the norms of their home countries. "My biggest shock was the realization that here people have too much freedom. There is no code. Some men wear long hair, [some] women shave their heads. That was both amazing and disturbing," recalls a student from a southern Indian province.

Having too many options to choose from is not always associated with anxiety and distress. For some individuals this experience may become stimulating and rewarding. "Moving from the British-African system of education to the United States was quite a surprise. We went from being slapped by a teacher for having your hands in your pockets to the environment where people do not seem to care what you wear to school. In Zim (our abbreviation for Zimbabwe) we were required to spend at least five hours on homework each weekend." (K. K., 21, student). "What I was surprised [about] the most was freedom of speech in classes," suggested a 35-year-old college professor, born in Egypt, who completed his education in New York. "I sometimes felt embarrassed to hear the students' questions and comments, sometimes about intimate topics, but mostly about the government. Students called professors by their first names and, on many other occasions, some students showed disrespect to their teachers. And that was almost a norm. I felt very uncomfortable during my first year as a student." For others, the existing freedoms cause an entirely

> ## A topic to think about
>
> Sometimes, culture shock may be a motivational, positive experience. Below is an excerpt from an interview. M. R., 25, born in Greece: "My first year in Los Angeles was like a football match to me, when your team is winning. Everything was great. I was excited since I planned my arrival here for a long period of time. I was finally free, and my head full of plans and projects. Everybody was helpful to me. During the first year, I learned a lot, everything was interesting, and I kept staring at many things with my eyes wide open."
>
> **Question:** What was your most pleasant experience during the first three months of life in the United States?

different psychological experience, like in this man from Bangladesh: "My shock was obvious. Coming from a highly regimented culture, I was overwhelmed with freedom that literally crushed on my shoulders. I didn't know what to do with it. One of the most amazing and difficult things was overcoming problems to choose: there were many available options here in America."

After you read these pages, could you describe what culture shock is? Is it a personal problem or personal growth? Is it a learning experience or loss of control over life events? Indeed, for some individuals, their initial stages of adjustment are remembered as the most exciting period of their lives, whereas for others it was interpreted as a fearful journey into the unknown. For some people, their culture shock is an anticipated relief, but for many others it is a road with thousands of abrupt curves and obstacles. For some, culture shock is nothing but pain and grief. For others it is just a stressful period of learning. The problem with the existing explanations of culture shock is that, in fact, different types of culture shock were described by different individuals who were going through different stages of their culture shock and were affected by different social and psychological conditions. For example, culture shock experienced by a refugee from Sudan, a mother of two, might be totally different than the culture shock experienced by a Brazilian or German exchange student.

It is true that understanding of a problem alone may not change a problem. Understanding is a first step toward creation of practical solutions. There are such solutions. There are ways to overcome culture shock if it occurs. The next topic will teach you how to manage culture shock. Let us examine some of the existing ways of effective adjustment to a new cultural environment. Do not forget that there is no single and universal procedure for culture-shock reduction. Every person chooses his or her own way.

CHANGE YOUR THINKING

As an Irish proverb says, if God shuts one door, he opens another. It would be so nice to discover these open doors for all people. In reality, many of us face only those doors that have been shut. And this is the problem. Psychologists suggest that not the events around us but also our irrational thinking about the events (when one sees only the shut doors, for example) causes psychological problems. Cognitive therapists share this view and believe that events in themselves do not cause negative emotions. Instead, frustration and anger, grief and anxiety are mainly due to our pessimistic description of events (Ellis, 1962). From this standpoint, culture shock can be interpreted as a result of a person's irrational thinking.

Let us consider the following example. Albert G., a 22-year-old exchange student, arrived in the United States six months ago. From the beginning of his life here, he has been experiencing symptoms of disappointment and persistent anxiety. He was also overwhelmed with pessimistic thoughts. According to the approach we are using now, Albert's symptoms should not be interpreted as negative developments caused by his arrival to a new country. The fact that culture shock follows migration doesn't prove that migration is the cause of culture shock. Likewise, the winter doesn't cause the spring just because the spring follows the winter! Therefore, we should try to give a different interpretation of the causes of Albert's culture shock. For instance, as Albert explained to us, he was always a disciplined boy and young man who would like to plan everything in his life and tried to achieve perfection in every endeavor. Moving to the United States caused a disruption in his lifestyle when he, temporarily of course, became unable to control things and events around him. At the same time, Albert's habitual desire to be successful and, even perfect, caused his emotional displeasure: his grades at school were not as good as he wanted them to be. In his home country, he was able to achieve some important goals, and his college grades were perfect. In the new culture, his old stereotypical patterns of thinking no longer worked. What should he do?

Under these circumstances, Albert should change his irrational self-perception as a "successful individual within a perfectly organized environment" and accept a more rational view of life. This means that for the time of his initial adjustment—which may last for several months—he should accept a view that would suspend his previously held perceptions on his own success. All in all, he doesn't have to be perfect, successful, and mistake-free during the period of adjustment!

Sergei Tsytsarev, a professor and psychotherapist from Hofstra University, has told us that those newcomers who view their present life situation, including their culture shock, in a more rational way adjust better than those who view their life in predominantly irrational terms. Moreover, studies show that people who are aware of their own feelings can exert greater control over their reactions to events (Perls, 1973). Yes, it is possible to encourage an individual to take responsibility for his or her actions rather than blame other people or even the entire society for the misery and suffering they feel. As a Chinese proverb suggests, two-thirds of what we see is behind our eyes. Therefore, it is almost imperative to look around frequently. Sometimes we have to do this more often than we did in the past.

ACCEPT THE REALITY AROUND YOU

Other specialists believe that our psychological problems during culture shock are caused by our inability to come to grips with the changes that we cannot control. We always gain and lose things, we all go through easy and difficult periods of life—and we have to accept anything that happens. For many people, their culture shock is, in part, a nostalgic reaction to loss. We have chosen to be away from our homeland, relatives, and familiar places. For those who experience culture shock, the loss should be articulated and explained. This becomes one's rational understanding, agreement with, and acceptance of the loss: this is my life and I accept it as it is. One cannot step twice into the same river, pointed out the Greek philosopher Heraclitus. This remarkable idea was shared with the authors during an interview with a 30-year-old woman from Peru: "I only now realized that many of my unpleasant feelings of loss associated with Peru are, in fact, my sadness about my happy childhood. Once I was a girl and it was back in Peru. I will never become a child again. And all my happy recollections about my innocent life of a little girl are associated with my home country. Now I have learned to enjoy my age and understand that I will never become small again."

"The lowest ebb is the turn of the tide," wrote American poet Henry Longfellow, more than a hundred years ago. Accepting this wisdom, applying it to one's life may indeed become an inspiration. Self-encouragement may also exist for some people in the form of a specific plan in life. As a young man from India told us, "I overcame my culture shock because I knew what to do in my life: I had a goal to become a doctor." Others form a general attitude of being busy, as one of the interviewees said about her mother: "By deliberately keeping herself busy with her everyday work, she forgot the fact that she was alone in a faraway land." It is important to know, nevertheless, that self-encouragement may become ineffective if you do not have enough time or resources to overcome the problems that you face. Unrealistic expectations may cause significant problems in initial adjustment.

ACQUIRE A NEW ATTITUDE

"In the hour of adversity be not without hope, for crystal rain falls from black clouds," wrote Nizami, a great Persian poet. A recovery from culture shock can begin with self-evaluation. As a result of this self-evaluation, a healthier attitude can be adopted. Look around you and find those areas in which you feel your weakness! Your weakness can become your strength. How do you achieve this? By changing the way you think about yourself. For example, what if some people do not understand your English? You have time; self-improvement will follow, and very soon everyone will realize that you speak two languages fluently (both your native tongue and English), whereas most people around you speak only one! Some people think of you as a helpless foreigner? Again, in time you will be able to prove that you can become as successful as others. "I felt from the beginning I had to do twice as much as others were doing to prove myself as worthy as an American person." With a sparking smile, this businessman from Iran described how he was brought to the United States as a teenager. "I said to myself: you have to be twice as better as people around you, especially if you are a minority person," recalled a student from Liberia, commenting on his recovery from pessimistic thinking and fears that were haunting him for months after his arrival to these shores. It is unfair, of course, to do twice as much as others do in order to succeed. But while it takes years and even centuries to change an unfair social system, it may take significantly less time to change one's attitude on the personal level. Remember, self-encouragement is a source of inspiration.

Developing a healthy attitude is often a process of reevaluation of expectations. Unrealistic hopes could cause poor adjustment and prolong culture shock. "Many newcomers have to adjust their expectations. Many of us have false perceptions of what life is like in America. We watch films, read magazines, and when we come here we realize that it is less idyllic than we thought of it. Life in America is not *Bay Watch* adventures or an *Independence Day* fairy tale," a student from Greece explained. A student's expectations may seem reasonable at first. For example, a young woman from Nigeria anticipated that she would do fine in the United States because of her command of the English language, spoken since birth. She, however, was shocked to realize that people in a small Michigan town could hardly understand her because of her specific accent, even though she spoke grammatically correct English. This shocking disappointment was frustrating for the woman and attenuated her culture shock.

The acceptance of a new attitude or reevaluation of one's expectations won't happen overnight. But even these relatively lengthy processes may be accelerated. Take one step at a time. Do not rush, be patient. Instead of trying to solve everything at once, decide what is the most urgent problem for you and concentrate on that first. Here is how an Iranian man describes his strategy during his first college year in the States: "At the beginning when I came here, I was trying to solve my immediate problems. I didn't have any long-lasting problems that other people have because I tried to focus on my immediate things. My life was like a military operation: you do this, you solve that. I always tried to calculate my next step."

A class assignment

I placed a blank piece of paper before a student and said, "I've told you about culture shock. Now write down everything that bothers you in your present situation." I offered him a pen. "In each sentence," I continued, "describe the things that you want to have and the obstacles that prevent you from getting these things done." It took him a little time before he began to write with a smile. "I want to bring my family here but (he hesitated for a second) I cannot do it at this time," he looked at me and I nodded in response, "Fine, continue, please." "I do not like this weather but my education is the reason why I stay here. I would like to have many friends but I dislike some people around me. I need somebody to talk with about my personal things but I always have to speak English; I cannot express myself well in English." There were more things written on that page. "Now listen to this," I said and give him a red pen. "Take a look at the list and substitute each use of *'but'* with *'and'*. Just erase every *'but'* and insert *'and.'* So what do you have now?" After a minute, he started reading:

"I want to bring my family here and I cannot do it at this time. I do not like this weather and my education is the reason why I stay here. I would like to have many friends and I dislike many people around me. I need somebody to talk with about some personal things and I always have to speak English; I cannot express myself in English."

I continued: "You see, by making these simple substitutions, you just corrected the way you see some problems. Now you may see your problems not as dilemmas, but as things that coexist with other things! These different aspects do not seem like contradictions any longer and then you learn how to live with them. . . . " "I understand," he replied after reading the sentence again. "This looks nice on a piece of paper, but how can I act this way?" "Yes, it's difficult. But—" I smiled, *"and*—let me correct myself too because I cannot use *'but'*—it's a long way and you have to begin with small things. Just remember this list and repeat it to yourself once a day. Begin with a change in your mind."

Assignment: Repeat the procedure described in this case. Please write down four or five problems that bother, upset, frustrate you today. In each sentence, put a desirable outcome first, then write <u>"but"</u> and then describe what prevents you from getting what you want to have or do. After you finish the sentences, please erase every <u>"but"</u> and insert instead <u>"and."</u> Now can you see your problems differently? Discuss your notes in class.

Perhaps you will set high goals and ambitions, but remember to be realistic. Make one decision today, not two decisions, because the second one should be made tomorrow. Expect small successes, incremental achievements. Do not look at others who seem to be doing better than you are. People are different. You choose your own pace of moving ahead. As German poet Wolfgang Von Goethe wrote almost two hundred years ago, "What each day needs, that shalt you ask, each day will set its proper task." We think his poetic advice doesn't sound too antiquated for modern times.

MAKE THINGS MORE FAMILIAR TO YOU

Do not *wait* for things to become familiar. "All problems become smaller if you do not dodge them but confront them," said renowned American Naval officer, William Halsey. To articulate one's problem and adjust one's attitude is the first step toward problem solving.

According to Turkish folklore, a neighbor came up to Nasraddin Hodja (a popular hero of Turkish tales whose remarks opened this chapter) and complained that there was no sunlight in his house. "Is there any sunlight in your garden?" Hodja asked. "Yes, certainly," replied the man. "Then move your house into your garden," suggested Hodja. Of course one cannot bring his or her home, friends, and relatives to the United States and put them in houses on the same street. On the other hand, you can bring something from your home culture, and you can learn about what most Americans do. "You know how we took care of our holidays in America? We celebrated both Moslem and Christian holidays. Christmas? Easter? No problem," suggested a student who came here from Iran in the early 1990s. "We celebrate our [Moslem] religious holidays as religious events, and consider local [Christian] holidays as the time for fun, guests, and gifts."

Creating your own psychological environment is called by psychologists *the self-discovery method.* Here the individual should create his or her own social climate in which this person feels comfortable. Observing and celebrating traditional holidays, commemorating great leaders of your country, organizing special events and parties, may stimulate promotion of self-acceptance. Self-discovery should not lead to self-isolation, as sometimes happens. For example, we knew a person from England who could not manage to settle into American life at all. She felt desperately homesick and could not function in America, constantly complaining about culture differences between England and the United States.

The similarities and differences we find around us are based on our descriptions. Descriptions, in turn, are always made from a particular point of view. Try to change your point of view and you will see things differently. A change in the perception could lead to a more pleasant feeling. "I think that for people who came here from Iran just before the revolution, their culture shock wasn't so difficult to overcome. Despite many differences, these two cultures had many things in common," said A., a professional, who was brought here as a teenager right after the Iranian Shah gave up his power. "After you told me about the similarities, I began to discover that people in my country act in almost the same way as people in America," suggested a student from South Africa. Some may even compare their experiences back home to the experiences here, always trying to find a positive side in the new experiences. Look at an example of such comparison below:

> It was warmer in Iraq, but here I spend most of my time at home, in the office, or in the car. I do not feel cold in the winter.

> The food was spicier at home, but here I also can go to our ethnic restaurants and eat my favorite dishes; besides I can cook at home.

> Most of my friends and relatives are in El Salvador; but here I also have many friends and I even find sometimes than there are more of them than I would like to have.

Psychologists suggest that like our old models of thinking, our old problem-solving strategies do not necessarily work in new environments: when you are "prompted to behave in the new setting using back-home cues, you will most likely encounter trouble" (Brislin & Pedersen, 1976). Elizabeth Goldston, a professional translator, reminded us about the tale of Gulliver, a man who was cast adrift in open seas and finally came ashore in the Land of the Houyhnhnms. There he encountered a new and strange culture wherein his initial assumptions, based on his previous cultural experience, proved completely inaccurate. Like Gulliver, in the process of resettling elsewhere we may find that all our previously acquired cultural knowledge becomes a poor compass to guide us through the quicksand of unfamiliar mores and customs of the new society. This assumption does not mean that we shouldn't use our old models of behavior. The point is that we ought to use them critically. We may have to compromise, but finding a middle course is not always about giving up something. Rather, it is adding to your new conditions an environment in which you feel comfortable and can perform effectively. Some critics say that by doing this we keep one foot on one bank of the river while trying to reach the other bank with the other foot. We would say: "We are not trying to step over the river. We are building a bridge."

LEARN FROM OTHERS

Do not wait for others to teach you. One approach psychologists use is called *participant modeling*. It requires an individual to acquire social skills by performing adaptive behaviors. To manage culture shock effectively, we have to learn those behaviors that are healthy and useful for us today and get rid of those behaviors that are not useful. Using this approach, it would be inaccurate to suggest that "People who are pessimistic expect the worst." Instead: "People who expect the worst are pessimistic." Likewise, it is incorrect to say that people with culture shock experience anxiety based on their disappointment with the United States. Instead, we would say that those newcomers who are disappointed with their lives here are experiencing culture shock.

This method of thinking must be learned and applied to new experiences to achieve new behavior. There are other methods that can be adopted for culture-shock management. Most of these methods assume a similar foundation: psychological training, which produces not only greater knowledge but develops new adaptive skills in participating individuals. Training methods accelerate the process of adaptation and make our behavior more productive. "They chew a ton of wood for an ounce of honey," says a Turkish proverb about those who do not have such behavioral skills. There is wisdom in old proverbs.

Another beneficial technique is to surround ourselves with people during our initial adjustment. Provide yourself with a wide range of role models, find encouragement from others with similar problems who can provide you with assurance that your problems are not unique and give you the opportunity to try out a new behavior. "When I got my first job, my manager, who also had come to America just five years ago, helped me a lot. She began to push me to do particular things, to overcome fears that I thought were impossible to defeat. I started to change, I could feel it," recalls F. A., a student from Afghanistan.

This *social–relations technique* could be used on a college campus or a similar setting where a wide selection of individuals with the same types of problems is available. A meeting or a discussion on culture shock where people can meet one another, share their concerns, and learn that others have similar problems, could be helpful. The facilitator of such a meeting should be someone who has already overcome culture shock and is able to share with others his or her experiences. It may be desirable to hold such meetings on a regular basis. Finding that other people and social groups also have similar problems is often helpful. Finding other people with whom you may have some common interests could also reduce feelings of isolation.

Another very successful method is *social skills training.* In this method, people rehearse new behavior in group settings. The difference here is that the focus is mainly on learning specific skills and behavioral responses. Such things as making a phone call, purchasing a car, filling out an application may be successfully rehearsed with other people in role-playing situations. In real life we learn how to do these things either alone or with the help of our friends. We learn both from our own mistakes and from the experience of others. In a training situation, we also gain experience and learn from mistakes, but we do it in specially designed settings where mistakes will be immediately corrected.

This method could be very helpful in learning the language or improving conversational skills. For instance, you can learn a set of phrases that are adaptive to particular situations. You can learn how to say "no" without being disrespectful, how to make a request, or how to place a phone call. Such learned phrases help build confidence and allow you to be more relaxed. In one of our workshops, for example, newly arrived students learned with joy and smiles on their faces how to do a standard exchange of greeting between two Americans. If you are asked: "Hi, how are you?" Simply answer: "Thanks, I am fine. How about yourself?" And then when you hear: "Just fine, thanks," go your own way. This simple method allowed the students to rehearse a fundamental principle for a brief communication between two acquaintances, illustrating that a detailed explanation of how we "are" isn't really being sought when someone asks "How are you?"

The same technique may be used for more comprehensive learning experiences, such as learning what to do, what to buy, and what to wear when you are invited to a Christmas party or a wedding. Indeed, most of us learn about these things from real-life situations, but such structured learning, especially in cases of culture shock, may be an important step toward rapid acquisition of social skills.

FAMILY ENGAGEMENT

Sometimes, if the situation allows, it is possible for family members to help one another deal with culture shock. Family members may work together to provide a less painful process of initial adjustment, especially in cases of refugees or asylum seekers. The main goal of family engagement is to teach social skills and establish rules that all family members can follow (*Utne Reader*, January–February 1997, p. 62). One family member may have an easier and faster initial adaptation than the others in the same family. "It was still easier for me to go through culture shock than for my older family members, brothers and sisters, my parents especially," said B. T., an Afghanistan-born young woman. Such people may serve as "role models" for other members of the family. "We gained a lot from our mother who was an extremely strong person. She was able to be strong in a new environment," an Egypt-born engineer from Virginia praised his mother. "The problem is that many families are not as lucky as ours." Indeed, sometimes families are so preoccupied by their own problems, they cannot pay attention to the coping strategies of their relatives. Family engagement allows, at least in some cases, families to establish understanding and develop mutual concerns among the family members.

JUST ASK!

American culture may seem individualistic but when you need help, ask for it! As American philosopher William Hocking put it, "we cannot swing on the rope attached only to our own belt." We need something or somebody to hold on to. This may be different from what many people are used to in their homeland, where an old good friend will knock at your door because he or she feels that you need aid. Search for help; do not wait too long. We acquire our friends in our home countries naturally, through schools you went to and streets you played on. If you have arrived in the United States as an adult, you will have fewer friends than you might wish to have. Adults everywhere have already established their own circle of friends. It can be disappointing to wait in hopes that somebody will befriend you. You may have to make the first move and take this difficult step toward friendship. To paraphrase an old axiom, "If the mountain doesn't go to you—you go to the mountain."

One of the authors of this book grew up in a communist country and was persuaded by the media that Americans are greedy and heartless, that they never help their neighbors, and they often abandon their friends when they are helpless. He discovered, however, that this is not true. Without his new friends, their generous help, advice, and support, without their friendship, his culture shock could have been more difficult than it was.

REENTRY SHOCK

Many students who we interviewed for this book never anticipated that going back home, even for a brief visit, can also cause a culture shock. **Reentry shock** is the psychological term for the confusion and frustration that is commonly felt when exchange students and immigrants return for a visit to their home cultures (Taliercio, 1996). Similar to culture shock, the symptoms of reentry shock could be either pleasant or disturbing. Surprisingly, people are often less aware of the severity of the emotional stress or surprise because it takes place in a culture that is supposedly familiar. "I anticipated how strange it would be to visit my country after these many years, but I never thought it would be so difficult." This is a common reaction of many who visit their home countries after spending a significant amount of time in the United States. Reactions can be emotional, like the one we recorded from a woman born in Burma who returned for a visit after ten years: "The food was different, I had never tasted such awful food in my life. But the worse thing was the odors around me." These frustrations are not uncommon. People who have been abroad for a long time often forget how much they have harmonized their lifestyles and attitudes to the norms of the new culture, so going home, even for a visit, means experiencing an acculturation process in reverse. Many develop a sudden distaste for their own countrymen, claiming they either lack a "worldview" or concern themselves too much with trivialities.

Friends and family can also be the root of a great deal of frustration. Returnees often report losing patience with loved ones when they try to talk about their experiences, finding that "no one cares or understands who I am now and what I have learned." People may be surprised to find that their friends are not exactly how they left them. Their former "best friends" may have found new friends, and what they wear or like in music may be different, which can result in feeling left out. "I was different perhaps because of my music preferences, my interests, the words I used, and definitely my dress code. I was not Bolivian, I was American in their eyes" (Kimberly).

A benefit of reverse culture shock is that it can help individuals upon their return to the U.S. with their adjustment and may become a stimulator toward more rapid acculturation.

Have you experienced this type of reverse culture shock? If yes, what did you feel? Did your impression of your home country change after you spent some time in the United States?

D*ia (a nickname), 21 years of age, is an Asian-born female and part-time college student. She came to the United States 2 years ago with her parents. Both her parents are scientists. Dia has a brother who is a 15-year-old high school student. Dia's complaints and concerns are: her English progresses too slowly; she is often frustrated when she does not understand what other people are saying; she has no friends and, therefore, feels extremely lonely; she feels inferior; she believes she does not look like most of the people around her; she even thinks that she looks ugly; she misses her home country, however, does not want to go back; as a source of "escape," she keeps listening to her country's music, reads books in her native language, and watches TV news broadcasts in her native language. Dia wants to adjust, get rid of her anxiety, and overcome her fear of rejection by others, the painful emotions that she hadn't experienced in her home country.*

Recommendations for change: Dia needs to recognize that she is experiencing culture shock. She may be able to improve her situation by deciding to undergo the following changes: First, Dia could reduce her frustration and eliminate her fears by changing her attitudes using social skills training. This technique can rid her of the stimuli that causes her negative tendencies; and help her acquire stimuli that will develop feelings of self-respect and personal satisfaction. Below are some behavioral modification techniques that may be helpful.

1. *Dia should speak English whenever possible, even at home with her parents and her brother. The more she speaks, the less reluctant to speak she will become.*
2. *Dia should feel free to ask people to repeat what they say to her. There is nothing embarrassing about asking someone to repeat themself. There are situations in which U.S. born and raised individuals sometimes do not understand one another.*

Question: *Continue to compile this list of recommendations for Dia. What would you advise her to do and how could she achieve these changes?*

Part Two

Strategies for Successful Students

Chapter 4
Communicating
with Professors

Remember your favorite teacher—that magnificent person from your high school days? Why did you like him or her? In all probability, you may have enjoyed this person's teaching style. Most of us like the way our favorite teachers speak, describe, and explain the material. Moreover, we know how to talk to them, when to ask questions, and how to make certain requests. All in all, we feel happy and comfortable with them. Wouldn't it be a wonderful idea to have this teacher in all your classes?

Let us get back to reality. We move, change schools, and change teachers. We must adjust to new people, their style and method of teaching, understand their requirements, and learn how to communicate with them. The situation becomes more difficult for those who continue their education in a new country. In the United States, there is great emphasis on diversity and multiplicity of styles; we must adjust to professors whose teaching methods, overall attitudes, and ways of communication can be as far apart from one another as are the North and South Poles. You cannot expect professors to change their style and be in some way similar to each other and your expectations. What we must do is adjust to and know how to interact with our college professors. Such knowledge comes with experience, of course. However, there are some basic cultural rules of interaction that every student ought to know. Some of the rules are cross-cultural. In other words, they may exist in each and every country in the world—and you will find out how similar these rules are.

There are, however, some practices that are culture-specific and must be learned and understood. This chapter will help you gain knowledge about some of the cultural rules that regulate communications between students and their professors in the United States.

ACCEPT DIFFERENT STYLES AND TRY TO COMMUNICATE

Simone was not very happy with the professor who taught her U.S. History class. She went directly to the history department chair to talk about this course and the professor who was teaching it. When the chairperson asked what was the problem, Simone's reply was that the professor did not follow the textbook precisely in his lectures. He would ask students to read the text at home; in class, however, the professor would teach material that was not in the textbook. Meanwhile, the professor also said the exams would cover both the lectures and textbook. Simone was confused. When the chairperson asked the student if there was anything she wanted to change, the student answered that she wanted the professor to change his teaching style and follow the textbook precisely.

Question: *Will Simone succeed in her request? Why or why not?*

Many exchange students report that they are surprised to learn how different and diverse college professors can be when one compares their teaching styles, grading policies, and general way of thinking. Indeed, all professors are different in terms of how much homework they assign, how much work is required in class, and how well they cooperate with students. A rule established by one professor—like submitting your homework assignments only in double spaced format—may not be required by another one. There are professors who will require you to do a substantial amount of reading and preparation at home so that you come to class prepared. During lecture, these instructors may occasionally refer to the text, but will mostly talk about things that do not appear in the textbook. On the other hand, there are professors who follow the textbook page-by-page and will not get far from its contents.

You will meet professors who give you the freedom to choose the best strategy for studying for their classes. Then again you will see professors who will follow a very strict and narrow set of procedures and will demand absolute discipline and organization from you. Some professors allow their students to improve their grades during the semester. For example, if you take several tests, the lowest score or grade will be eliminated. These professors will offer extra-credit assignments and offer make-up exams that could boost your grade. Others will not offer any make-up tests or extra-credit work and will never eliminate the lowest test grade. Some professors do not give any credit for attendance, suggesting that being in class is your choice. Others give credit for attendance, which may be critical for your final grade.

In general, professors follow majors guidelines for classroom instruction. You should not anticipate that every professor will use the same method of teaching. Therefore, in the case described earlier, Simone cannot anticipate that the department chair would tell the professor how she is supposed to teach her classes and what topics should be included or excluded from lectures. Is there a solution for Simone? Yes, there is. If she prefers to study by the book, she can find another professor who also prefers this type of teaching.

TALKING AND DISCUSSING

Hanna, a student from a Middle Eastern country, has taken three classes with Professor James over a one-year period. When the semester was over Hanna came to Professor James' office to learn about her grade. "It is interesting," commented the professor. "I now realize that I haven't heard your voice the entire year, not during class discussions, nor after class." Hanna smiled in reply: "Yes, I don't talk much."

Question: Do you think that Hanna's "quietness" was due to her individual style, or is it more likely to be a cultural pattern of behavior typical in many other foreign students?

Some international students remain silent in class and do not participate much in discussions. This can be for a number of reasons. Some students believe that their knowledge of the English language is not good enough and they do not want to embarrass themselves when speaking in front of the class. Others think that they do not know enough about the lecture's subject. Some say that they do not talk much due to cultural rules of their own country, such as questioning a person of higher social rank, which may be considered discourteous.

In the United States, however, talking to your professor and asking questions is considered a good sign of your interest in the subject. Moreover, your professors are constantly encouraged to communicate with the students. If you do not want to speak up in front of everybody, talk to the professor after class. If you have several questions and need some detailed comments, ask the professor for a meeting during his office hours. If you want to share your concerns about the class, go ahead. Your critical suggestions will not be considered a sign of disrespect to your instructor.

Try to participate in class discussions or ask questions. Such participation will not only improve your communication skills and increase your self-confidence, it will also help professors to explain the topic clearly. Do not be afraid to talk to a professor even if you think that the subject of your conversation might not be very important to him or her. Say "hello" to your professors when you see them in the library, cafeteria, hallway, or on the street, even though you do not have anything to discuss. Just a smile can make a difference in someone's mood. Remember your teachers are human beings and they have their own concerns, make mistakes, may have good and bad days. They, too, need support, and many of them will appreciate it if you

A topic to think about

Can your boss be wrong? This case was covered in major newspapers around the world. The copilot and engineer of Korean Air flying a Boeing 747 discovered that something was wrong with the flight: all indicators suggested a problem. However, neither man said anything about the problem to their captain, who apparently did not see any danger. Several seconds later, the airplane slammed into the top of a mountain, killing 228 passengers. Investigators established that the crew failed to challenge the captain, showing a traditional respect for authority in command. In other words, they assumed that if the boss did not see the problem, then there was no problem (Phillips, 1998). Of course, your classroom is not an airplane and your professor is not a commander. However, such an attitude may be shared by some students: the professor is always right because he or she is a teacher. What do you think about such an attitude? Can you recall situations when your teacher made a mistake? Did you tell anybody about that mistake? Do you remember occasions when you disagreed with your professor? Did you express your disagreement? Please explain.

express your interest, for example, in their research. It is proper to ask questions about where and when they earned their degrees, what is their current research topic, and what is the next academic conference they are going to attend. You may ask your teachers about their families. There is a simple test: if you see that your instructor is willing to talk about his family and children, you can continue the conversation. If he does not want to talk about these topics at length, please understand and avoid asking further personal questions.

BRINGING GIFTS

Arra wanted to thank his English literature professor for a great semester. The best way to express his appreciation—Arra thought—would be giving something memorable to the professor. A gift is a sign of gratitude and respect. It always reminds people about you and makes them feel special. Coincidentally, Arra's mother was in the United States at that time, visiting with her son on campus. She brought from her home country a stunning hand-made quilt beautifully decorated with national ornaments. "That would be a perfect gift," Arra thought. "The semester is almost over and the professor will be very happy to have this quilt." Next morning Arra called the professor to make an appointment with him.

Question: *Would you approve or disapprove of the student's decision to bring the quilt to the professor as a gift?*

It is a fine idea to want to express your appreciation to someone who has spent many hours in the classroom sharing with you her knowledge and skills. Are there any customs and rules that regulate the ways you should express your thanks to your teachers? What are the most and least appropriate ways to convey your gratitude to the professor?

If you really enjoyed the semester, you can simply stop by the professor's office and say a few nice words about the course. Some students like to sign a card with a few words of appreciation in it. A postcard with a picture of your hometown or country would be a fine token of respect. There are students who bring samples of their ethnic food to share with their teachers. A simple written note, however, will always be an appropriate sign of appreciation.

Never bring expensive gifts. Giving presents is a tradition that exists in every country. However, people also follow certain rules about giving gifts at work. Such rules of ethical behavior do not encourage American college professors to receive gifts from their students. The professor may feel it necessary to refuse to accept your gift, and that can be an embarrassing situation for both of you. A student, with the best intentions, may insist that the gift indicates his deep feeling of gratitude to the teacher, which is understandable. However, professional rules of teacher–student communication are different from those that friends establish among themselves. Any gifts offered by a student to the professor ahead of final grades could be considered bribes. Moreover, other students may think of a gift-giver as someone who wants to earn an easy grade with the "purchasing power" of her contributions. Therefore, if the professor refuses to accept a gift, it doesn't mean that he is disrespectful to the student. The teacher is simply following professional rules of conduct. What should you do if you really want to express your thankful thoughts to the instructor? The answer is: your sincere words. They will mean more to your professor than any souvenirs.

What will be reasonable advice to give to Arra regarding that expensive quilt brought from his home country? The answer: do not present it to your professor; give it to a good friend of yours instead!

TO INVITE OR NOT TO INVITE?

Next week Roberto and Maria—second-year exchange students and twins—celebrate their 20th birthday. They invited several friends to their birthday party, mostly their fellows from the university. Prior to sending invitations, Roberto and Maria argued about whether or not it would be appropriate to invite their favorite math professor. Roberto pointed out that this professor was always open-minded and friendly with students. However, the semester was far from over. If he were invited, some of the other students might consider the invitation an attempt to get a break in the forthcoming tests.

Question: *What should they do: invite or not invite the professor to their celebration?*

Most of us want to share our joy with people we like. In every country, it is natural to invite those people to celebrate good news (and sometimes grieve over bad news) with us. We commonly invite our relatives, friends, and sometimes strangers to share a moment of joy. Would it be a good idea to invite a favorite professor to celebrate with us? The answer is: of course, you can invite anyone you like. However, such informal contacts between students and professors are not always appropriate. Why? Because the professor should not show any favoritism to particular students. There are certain formal and informal rules that American professors must follow in their daily interactions with students.

For example, it would be appropriate to invite an instructor to nearly any organized event on campus. It is always a good idea to send an invitation in advance—at least two or three weeks before the event takes place—so that the invitee is able to include this event in his or her work schedule. Celebrations such as a national holiday, a religious holiday, an important national date that commemorates your country's history, all are appropriate reasons for inviting some of your professors for a meeting or party. A more delicate situation can occur, however, if a celebration is held in your dormitory, apartment, house, picnic area, restaurant, or any other place off-campus. Professors, of course, are the ones to make a final determination about what is proper and what is not, and will make the final decision about whether to attend a celebration.

Certain events will, of course, take place without the presence of faculty members, because these events are expected to be private. Among these events are: your own birthday or birthday of your boyfriend, girlfriend, husband, or wife; arrivals or departures of your relatives (even though they might insist on meeting with your professors); and any of your "regular" parties that you organize for almost no reason. On the other hand, it is always a fine idea to invite faculty members to attend a sports game. Some professors never miss the opportunity to play basketball, soccer, or football with their students. Do not forget about chess or other board games.

As to Roberto and Maria's dilemma, good advice might be to let their professor know that they are going to celebrate their 20th birthday. Rather than request your professor's presence at the party, invite your friends instead.

TO CONTACT OR NOT TO CONTACT?

Shandra is a very happy person, outgoing and optimistic. She enjoys her study in America, has many wonderful friends, is always ready to help when somebody needs her assistance or just kind words. She likes to share good news with friends and usually spends at least one hour a day sending and receiving email messages. She has several mailing lists. One contains the names of her parents and other family members in Brazil. Another list contains names of her friends, former classmates in several countries around the world. Her third mailing list contains names of her friends and acquaintances from school. Shandra loves to send copies of messages to everyone on her mailing lists with recent updates, jokes, interesting pieces of information, discussion topics, and some news that she thinks is related to business administration—her major and future specialty. Recently she added to this list several names of her favorite professors, who Shandra thinks would enjoy reading her messages.

Question: *In your opinion, was it a good idea to add the names of her professors to one of her mailing lists?*

Although the good old telephone today remains a very important source of communication, American professors in increasing numbers are using email to exchange information and news. Only a few years ago this form of communication was considered entertaining and amusing. But that has changed. Today it is becoming increasingly difficult to use email because there are too many messages being received and not enough time to go through all of them! On an average day, a college professor receives from 7 to 10 electronic messages from colleagues and school administrators. Moreover, if a professor teaches three classes with 30 students each, her potential for messages can be in the hundreds daily. How can you be "email effective"—in other words, how can you get the most from your electronic communication with professors? There are several tips that can make your interpersonal communications more efficient.

If you have questions to your professor about the course you are currently taking, please make sure that these questions are not already answered in the syllabus or other course documents. If you have a question about a recent lecture, be sure that the question is short so that the answer, too, can be brief. Unless your professor has agreed to discuss some topics with you at great length, please respect his time: sometimes it is easier and takes less time to ask a question and receive an answer in person. To simplify the professor's work, always design your letter so that the professor can easily recognize who the sender is.

A common communication error that many students commit is displayed in the following example:

"Professor, this is J., we spoke today; I'm taking your class. Will you be so kind and tell me my grade for the last test?"

Even though the professor recognizes your face, it is quite likely that she may not remember what class you are taking, especially if she teaches two or three sections of the same course. Therefore, at the beginning of the message, please put your name, the course you are taking, including the course section and the time the class meets. Try to ask questions about your grade when the professor has easy access to the grade book or the computer file. Sometimes it can be done more efficiently in person after class or during office hours.

Every professor will probably explain what kind of electronic communication he expects to establish with the students during the semester. Some professors allow students to request their grades via email. On the contrary, some could ask you to do it in person during office hours. Some professors will not mind sending you copies of class assignments and other handouts distributed in class. Others will not do that under any circumstances. In any case, if you have doubts about the professor's style of communication, ask this question after class or send a message. Your professor will appreciate such a request.

Try to understand that in the vast majority of situations, your electronic communication with professors should be formal. It is different from your electronic interaction with friends to whom you can send

For class discussion

Consider the following message left on a professor's answering machine:

"Hello, professor, this is Ahmad calling; could you tell me what is the status of my request? We spoke yesterday and you asked me to call today."

Can you find several mistakes that Ahmad made in his assertion? First, he did not mention his last name. The second error is that Ahmad failed to remind the professor of the nature of the request. The professor may remember his conversation with Ahmad. Nevertheless, it is helpful to remind the person of the topic of your previous conversation and the nature of your request. Imagine, for example, the following case. You are going to pick up your friend at the airport tomorrow and will have to miss a test. You talked to your professor in advance and she asked that you call her today to clarify what you are supposed to do about the missed exam. Compose an "ideal" telephone message you would leave on the professor's answering machine.

messages spontaneously as soon as you have an idea in your hand. Please do not send your professor any jokes, funny stories, and other interesting—from your viewpoint—pieces that are flying in cyberspace. If you think that you have found an extremely interesting piece of information, save it on disk first, and then tell your professor about it. If he is interested, then send this piece over. If you need your professor's suggestions or other help, it is always better to make an appointment rather than send an email. During the appointment, the teacher can spend more time and can offer you more options than she or he can via email.

We would advise Shandra not to include her professors' names in her mailing lists. If she really wanted to do this, she should ask their permission first. It is important to respect other peoples' privacy.

RULES OF ADDRESS

The door to my office was open but the student knocked anyway. "May I come in?" he asked cautiously. "Yes," I replied. "Come in, sit down please. How can I help you?" The student entered my small office, smiled, and said quietly: "Dr. Eric, I have a question for you." The question was simple and I quickly gave the answer. What was interesting about the situation was the way the student addressed me. He called me "Dr. Eric." That's a form of address I haven't heard very often. Maybe my last name is too difficult to pronounce correctly? Or maybe it is not difficult to articulate but difficult to remember? Or, is this a new, popular style of address?

Question: *Is it appropriate to address your professor by his or her first name?*

Some students are uncertain about how to address their professors. Does one have to use their first name, or last name, or maybe both? How can one use academic and professional titles when addressing other people? In addition, for some students it may become tough to pronounce some professors' last names. If a name is difficult to pronounce, the situation creates additional difficulties: fear of embarrassment, fear of rejection, and worry about possible criticism.

Not many professors in the United States who teach undergraduate students prefer to be called by their first names: John, Barbara, or Henry. Under most circumstances it is preferable to use your teacher's last name, regardless of how difficult it may be to pronounce. If your professor is a man, you can call him Mr. Browning or Mr. Wong. If your professor is a woman, you should call her Mrs. Smithers (if she is married) or Ms. Nicholson. If you do not know her marital status, you should use Ms. in your address. There are gender-neutral forms of communication. For example, you can freely call your instructor "professor" and include the last name, for example, Professor Gonzales. If the instructor has a doctorate degree, it is common to call him or her "doctor," again including the last name: Doctor Barnard or Doctor Bean, which is the preferable address.

Many students—especially from Arab countries—use the instructor's title and first name. For example, they would say "Dr. John" or "Professor Susan." This is not a common form of address in direct communications, although it is likely to be accepted by most professors.

When you start a conversation or want to get your instructor's attention, bear in mind that you are not talking to a stranger. Introductory words such as "excuse me" or "wait a minute" are not the best starters for you conversation with any professor. It is always a sign of respect to use the name of your professor or his title when addressing him. For example, you can say, "Excuse me, Professor Fukuda" or "I have a question, Doctor Deregowski."

Pay attention to how your teacher's name is spelled. Most professors will not pay special attention to whether or not you correctly spell their names in your written reports; however, some instructors are very sensitive to how their names appear on paper or in an electronic message. So double-check the spelling of your instructor's name on your assignments or written messages.

When you call your professor on the phone, always say your name and the class you are taking (do the same in your email messages). Remind the person you are calling of the nature of your question or request.

PERSONAL PROBLEMS: TO SHARE OR NOT TO SHARE?

When Tina appeared in the professor's office she was visibly upset. Moreover, when Tina began to talk, her voice was breaking and she was about to cry. "Professor," she said, "I need your help and advice. My parents want me to get back to my home country because they think that my education is not going well here. I am not getting good grades and this is the only thing they care about. They do not care about how I would feel if I leave this place. I made so many great friends *here. I know that I can improve the grades very soon; but it takes time, and my parents do not want to wait. Please tell me what to do: to oppose my parents and stay here or get back to my home country? Please let me know; I really like your lectures."*

Question: *Is Tina making a wise decision by talking to her professor about a private issue? Does a college professor have an obligation to help students who experience personal problems?*

When there is a tough decision to make, many people usually seek help and advice from their relatives and close friends. However, when you live away from home you may not have many people who you can talk to and share your concerns, pain, or to whom you can simply complain about something you dislike. Generally speaking, if a problem occurs, try to talk to the person who you think is able to solve this problem. For example, if you think that your math professor did not grade your exam justly, the first step is to speak to the professor in person and ask her to explain how your test was graded. After such a conversation—in most cases—the problem is solved: the professor may find an error in grading or explain to you why you received this particular score. If you are still not satisfied with the way your problem is being solved or your request is handled, you can speak to one of the college's supervisors. Almost every employee on campus, including faculty members, has a supervisor who is supposed to help you solve the problem, if it persists.

Almost every professor will be willing to listen to you carefully and offer practical help or an advisory opinion. You have to differentiate, however, between at least two types of problems that you may encounter, which require two different approaches to the solution. First, there are problems—formal or organizational—that can and should be solved by college administration, not by one of your professors. Certain rules and standard procedures need to be followed when those solutions are offered. Second, there are personal problems that are mostly concerned with interpersonal relationships with the people in your life. Refer now to the box below, read the scenarios, and decide which are "official" and which are "personal."

Did you determine that situations 1, 3, and 5 are "personal" problems? You can talk about them to your professor, but do not anticipate that he will give you a suggestion about what to do. He is not in a position to give you advice. Therefore, do not anticipate that your professor will say a lot to a question related to your relationship with your parents, siblings, or friends. The student counseling center

A class assignment

Please indicate which of the problems below are "official" and should be addressed through official channels at your college, and which of them are "personal." Discuss your answers in class.

1. You have already broken up with your friend and need your professor's advice on whether to see this person again.
2. You got a parking ticket and you do not want to pay it because you think that campus police gave you the ticket by mistake. You ask your professor to intervene and help you resolve the situation.
3. Your parents told you to select computer science as your major. However, you want to choose biology. What can you do in this situation? You ask your professor what major you should declare.
4. You have a problem with a student who verbally assaulted you not long ago and threatened to create more problems for you in the future. You ask your professor's advice.
5. You have a problem with your roommate. She is messy, noisy, and always talks to you when you are working on homework assignments. You ask your professor to have a word with your roommate.
6. The library wants you to pay a fine for returning a book past its due date. You ask your professor to resolve the situation.

is the best place to seek help related to your personal problems. Situations 2, 4, and 6 require some "formal" action to resolve them. Your instructor can tell you what "official" channels you should use, and can help you find the right office where you should go.

What kind of personal information can you disclose to your college professor, and should you expect help in these situations? Professors are not permitted to share with anyone else any private information you disclose to them. Feel free to tell them what you feel is appropriate to tell. Understand, however, that professors are not marriage counselors or psychotherapists (although some of them may hold these titles). The most a professor can do is to listen to you and give a general opinion. Of course, they will be happy to give a more specific suggestion if your request is a course-related one. Ask them what book to buy or what article to look for, and they will be happy to elaborate on that subject.

NEGOTIATING YOUR GRADE

Palar was disappointed with the grade he received for his sociology class. At the beginning of the semester he anticipated receiving an "A." When the grades were posted, he found that he was given a "C." Palar decided to talk to the professor. Reason? He didn't like the grade. He knew that during the semester he was not getting good test scores in this class. He also remembered he missed several classes that could also have lowered his grade. Nevertheless, Palar was very optimistic about having a conversation with the professor. He knew that he could do much better in this class. He also knew he was a great negotiator. In his home country, his teachers told him many times that he could become a fine businessman because he knew how to bargain. In his brief career he had learned to negotiate almost anything, anywhere: at a farm market, car dealership, travel agency, and many other places. Palar thought that if he asked the professor to change the grade from a "C" to an "A," after some negotiation, the professor would give him a "B."

Question: Is it a good idea to discuss your grade with a professor, or is it absolutely inappropriate?

Some people mistakenly presume that a college education is a kind of business and professors are entrepreneurs who "take" money from students and "give" an education and grades in exchange. Some believe that for the money students give for their education they are entitled to negotiate the outcome, i.e., the grades. It is not that Palar cannot ask his professor why the grade was a "C." Moreover, professors usually keep students informed about their grade status throughout the semester. In this case, Palar knew that his class performance was far from satisfactory. However, he believed, that like everything else in life, his grade could be negotiated. Through the use of his communication skills and a great deal of aggressiveness, he anticipated that he could persuade the professor to change the grade.

Palar has made a mistake to assume that college grades can be bargained between students and professors. The rules are fair and square: grades are not supposed to be negotiated. Professors give grades according to their grading system, not according to what their feelings are or what some students tell them they want to get. If a student believes that there is a computation error in the professor's calculations, she should mention it and ask the teacher to set aside a few minutes and recalculate the grade. For this purpose, keep copies of your graded tests and homework assignments. There cannot be any other reasons, however, for you to ask your professor to change your grade.

A topic to think about

Below are reasons that some students give for trying to negotiate their grades with the professor. Please take a look at the explanations and see why these reasons cannot be accepted as legitimate requests for a grade change.

- *Professor, I attended all your lectures, submitted all the required assignments, and took all the tests. However, my grade is not an "A." I think I deserve a better grade.* **Why the grade will not be changed:** Even though one takes all the tests and fulfills all the requirements for the course, the final grade is based on the quality of the submitted assignments and tests, not on one's positive attitude and good intentions. There are plenty of sports teams, as an example, that play all the games but still may finish last in the season.
- *Professor, I never get grades lower than "A" (or "B"). Therefore, I should receive an "A" ("B") in your class too.* **Why the grade will not be changed:** Your past performance is not necessarily an indicator of what grade you will achieve in your next class.
- *Professor, this semester was very difficult for me. I was taking five classes. I did not have much time to prepare for the tests in your class. However, I enjoyed your teaching method and I think I really improved my skills and acquired new knowledge. I think I can improve my grade if you give me an extra week.* **Why the grade will not be changed:** Every student has the choice before the semester begins to take more or fewer classes. You are responsible for the additional pressure you placed on yourself by taking more classes than you could handle. In addition, by requesting an extra week, the student is asking for a break that the other students will not have.
- *Professor, without a good grade in your class, I will not be able to apply for graduate school (transfer to another school; apply for financial aid; etc.). Please understand my situation and change my grade.* **Why the grade will not be changed:** Colleges and universities are not designed to give away grades because someone wants to go to a different school or pursue a particular career. If one's grades are lower than he expected them to be, he can always retake some of the classes to improve the grades.

KEEPING APPOINTMENTS

Robert was very interested in the history of the American Revolution. He came to his professor and said he would like to learn more about this period in history. He also said that he might think about majoring in history. The professor said he would be very happy to chat with Robert tomorrow afternoon during lunch. The professor made an appointment to meet with Robert in the cafeteria at 12:40 P.M. the next day. Robert agreed to be there. Robert could not have anticipated how busy he would be the next morning. When he ran to meet his professor, he realized he was late. He was thinking: "If I'm late 10 or 20 minutes, that will be okay. The teacher is a junior professor and it is no problem to be late for a meeting with him. One has some time flexibility with the middle-aged professors; and one has to be very careful and try not to be late for meetings with senior professors."

Question: What was correct and incorrect in Robert's thinking?

The word *appointment* is very popular in America. Listen to what other people say and you will hear this word mentioned very often in their conversations. From the beginning of their lives, people in the United States are taught to schedule appointments. If you want to meet someone and discuss business or business-related problems, you typically have to agree on both the place and the time of such a meeting (see Chapter 3 on Culture Shock). Some professors do not have to schedule appointments with their students because they can receive students only during office hours.

Professors do more than teach classes. Their day is filled with various activities, from preparation and reading of new literature related to their classes, to grading papers and exams and reviewing lecture notes. Most professors have scholarly research to do. Some do their research in their offices; some of them spend a substantial amount of time in the library; some of them have to go off-campus. Professors also attend meetings, meet with other professors and school officials, write reports, and help graduate students and guest scholars. Therefore, it is highly unlikely that your professor will be able to talk to you whenever you show up at his or her office; you must have an appointment.

The most convenient time for you to talk to the professor, of course, is either before or after class. It is probably not a good time for her, however, unless she has scheduled office hours at that time period. It is easy to understand why. Right before class, the instructor would like to think about the lecture; read over any new information; make copies and prepare handouts and other class materials. In addition, the professor may have plans after class, so they can answer your questions only briefly. To avoid confusion or disappointment, always ask the professor if she has some time available for you and your questions. Do not keep your professor long after class, unless he has said it is all right. Your teacher may have another class or an important appointment in several minutes.

Robert's "theory" about how late he could be for the appointment being dependent upon status, disregards simple rules of courtesy. Regardless of your professor's age and rank, if you show up just one minute past the appointment time, you are late.

Think critically

If you ask several people who have traveled around the world about how people treat time in various countries, they will say that there are differences. One of our friends from the Caribbean said recently that, on his island, people are generally not in a hurry. Compared to Americans, they have a broader definition of being "late" for an appointment or meeting. We asked 129 students the following question: "Imagine the following situation. You are hosting an afternoon meeting with student delegates from four countries: Japan, Italy, Russia, and Germany. They all arrived yesterday and are staying in different hotels downtown. Using common expectations, hypothesize about which of the delegates will arrive on time and which will be more likely to arrive late for the meeting?" Of the answers we received, 97 students suggested that both German and Japanese delegates were likely to be on time; 103 answers indicated that both Russians and Italians might be late (Shiraev & Levy, 2000). We could say, however, that what we measured here are people's stereotypes about other countries.

Of course, there are studies that examine perception of time directly. For instance, students from Brazil and California were asked to explain the meaning of the phrase "being late." The average Brazilian student defined *lateness* for lunch as $33^1/_2$ minutes after the scheduled time, compared with 19 minutes for the American students. Brazilians also allowed an average of about 54 minutes before they would consider someone early, while the American students drew the line at 24 minutes. Unlike their American counterparts, the Brazilian students believed that a person who is consistently late is probably more successful than one who is consistently on time (Levine & Wolff, 1992).

Even though cultural differences in time perception exist, one can argue that many contemporary technological developments, including the expansion of television and the Internet, as well as the increasing complexity of modern life, should make cultural differences in how people perceive time less significant than they have been in the past. Do you think that in the contemporary world people treat their time more or less in the same way? Do you think that, instead of emphasizing cultural differences, we can see that there are different individual characters in every culture: there are people who are precise and disciplined, and there are those who are always late?

ASKING FOR A LETTER OF SUPPORT

*A**fter finishing her two-year education at a local college, Laura decided to transfer to a small private university. Before starting the transfer, she needed to collect a recommendation letter from one of her former professors. Laura decided to ask Professor Brown to write the letter because she did well in this professor's class. She checked Professor Brown's schedule and waited to talk to her near the classroom following an evening class she was teaching. After all the students were gone, she approached the professor with a smile, and said: "Professor Brown, do you remember me? Thank you, I have a favor to ask. I need a letter of recommendation from you. Can you give it to me on Monday? I know today is Friday; I hope it is enough time for you to write this letter. Thank you again."*

Question: *What mistakes did Laura make in her request for a letter of support from Professor Brown?*

When you plan to transfer to another college or want to apply for a job or for any other reason, you will need a recommendation letter, often called a "letter of support." Many students believe that to obtain such a letter, they must simply go to somebody they know and ask him to give them a recommendation. However, if your teacher agrees to give you this letter, you have to take some extra steps and help your professor to prepare a good document. Prepare a brief memo to your professor. It should contain the following items: your name, your major, the class or classes you are taking or have already taken with this professor, your major accomplishments, such as awards or achievements, and your professional experience—if any. Do not forget internships and other forms of activities. Inform them about where the letter is being submitted. Do not come with such a request on the same day you need the letter. Give your professor at least several days, and preferably a week, to prepare the letter.

RECORDING YOUR ACCOMPLISHMENTS

*E*va *was approached by a school official who said there was a job available for her next semester. It was a very desirable and long-anticipated job for Eva because she would work on campus and she could adjust her work hours to her class schedule. Eva was asked to prepare a resume. She was asked to include in the resume all her accomplishments and bring it in the next day. Eva went home and opened a new file on her computer. She began to realize how difficult it was to write about herself. Accomplishments? Achievements? There were so many interesting events in her life, but she seemed to have a hard time putting everything together.*

Question: *When should one start working on a resume?*

If you plan to continue your education or to work in the United States, you will need to have a resume or brief autobiography. Many students pay little or no attention to their resume until the time comes when they have to submit one. Certain rules apply when putting together a resume. Formal rules are readily available at the library or on the Internet. However, some students do not realize that a good resume takes more than a few minutes to prepare. Therefore, the process of resume writing can begin as early as your first day in college. Record in a notebook things that you do as a student. Write down information about awards you receive, concerts and sports tournaments you organize, student conferences you participate in, membership in student groups on campus, volunteer services, tutoring of other students, internships, and articles written. To be more competitive than other students, include specific results and accomplishments, not only the meetings you attend or groups in which you were just a formal member.

DETAILS, DETAILS, DETAILS . . .

Throughout this textbook the authors have strongly suggested that every student who goes through an adjustment period should look around and see what other people are doing. We often learn by imitation. Sometimes these lessons are great. Learning from others can be quick, useful, and profitable experiences. Sometimes, however, we observe wrong examples. Most students around you are mature, polite, considerate, and helpful. Nevertheless there are some students whose behavior should not be imitated. Below is a section of some practical suggestions about what is considered to be appropriate behavior that will help you to be effective in your interaction with faculty members.

- Never talk loudly with your friends in class during lecture. Exercise your freedom of expression when the professor asks you to express your opinion. Even though you think that you are not talking aloud, the professor can hear your conversation, which may disturb the lecture. Moreover, students who are sitting near you may also be disturbed by your chat. Remember, the classroom is for learning and not for exchanging comments about yesterday's game or your new friends.

- Everybody is very busy. We know that we are not supposed to be late for class. If you are late, try not to be disruptive. As you enter the classroom, do not walk slowly in front of the professor and the entire class. Try to avoid attention and find a seat in the corner.

- Never start your conversation with the professor by saying, "Hey, how did you like my last paper?" or "What can you say about my exam?" Most professors have good memories, however, they may not remember what you wrote in the last paper or what grade you got on the last test. For such questions, see the instructor in her office where she can easily check her record.

- If you make an important request to a professor, make it in writing—for example, if you need a recommendation, or want your professor to give you an extra-credit assignment, or you want to invite him to attend a celebration. Remember, a brief written memo in many situations is better than a long conversation.

- Try not to speak loudly with your friends in your native language in the presence of a professor with whom you are speaking. There is nothing wrong with speaking one's own language; however, when several people are holding a conversation, everyone is entitled to understand what the participants are saying. Speaking a language your teacher does not understand may be interpreted as disrespectful.

■ Many students grab something to eat before going to class. If your food contains fresh onion or garlic, consider eating it after you return home from school. Garlic and onion smell can be offensive and may distract people who you are talking to, including your professor. Professors may not mention your garlic or onion breath; however, they will run away from you.

A homework assignment

When we interact with other people we pay attention to how they use their bodies, hands, and faces to convey their thoughts and emotions. Psychologists suggest that the speaker's body language helps us understand this person better. Born in Mexico, India, Vietnam, or Indonesia—we understand many similar signs of body language (see Triandis, 1992). One quick smile and you understand that the professor is joking. A smirk may indicate that she is being sarcastic. By shrugging the shoulders, a person shows that he does not know something. There are differences, however, in how we use and position our bodies when we speak. Touching is more common in cultures around the Mediterranean Sea and in some Slavic nations than it is in the United States. Latinos may interact using smaller physical distances compared to people from Japan or East Asia.

Assignment: Observe your professors' movements, facial expressions, their entire "body language." See how they shift their eyes, where they point their finger, how often and how high they wave their arms, when they scratch their head, and so forth. Try to find similarities between how these people and people in your home country express themselves. Discuss your findings in class.

Chapter 5

Tips for Writing

America is a culture of written communications. Invitations, memos, announcements, and reminders are typed and placed daily into people's mailboxes or attached to bulletin boards. America is switching rapidly from telephones to email. People write to each other on Internet chatrooms. Written tests and written assignments are the core of the colleges' evaluation systems. Oral exams, often practiced in other countries, are administered in only a few schools in the United States. Perhaps your success in college will be measured, in part, by how well you write. In this chapter, we will explain how to prepare for written assignments and research papers. Here we discuss some important tips of successful paper writing and introduce several principles of analytical thinking—a key tool to effective discovery, examination, and interpretation of facts.

Written assignments are one of the most challenging activities in college. Do not get the impression that people who attended American elementary, middle, and high schools, who have spoken English since birth, have a tremendous advantage over you. Maybe sometimes it is easier for them to understand professors, take notes, and quickly grasp what is required in written assignments. It also appears that it is easier for them to put their thoughts into writing. But please do not be discouraged. You have both skills and opportunities to write well and be competitive. If you accept the following suggestions and work on your writing skills every day, you will definitely become a better student!

THE RESEARCH PAPER: PREPARATION STRATEGIES

When we write poetry we use a free flow of associations to link the images in a pleasing way. In verse, we convey our feelings and appeal to the feelings and imagination of the reader. A paper on history, sociology, psychology, political science, and many other subjects is quite a different activity. Professors normally provide you with some instructions and guidelines on what is expected in their writing assignments. Every professor may have a unique set of advice and recommendations to students. However, there are certain principles of paper-writing that most American professors expect every student to follow. Thus, for most assignments, you will be asked to work independently and to express your independent judgment based on empirical materials available to you, including confirmed facts, statistical information, expert judgment, opinion polls, and other data. It is also commonly anticipated that your research paper will be a rational and critical evaluation of the suggested topic. It is expected that you cite references, i.e., name the source of your facts. If you do not cite references, it is considered to be plagiarism. Most colleges and universities have harsh penalties for this kind of cheating. We will further discuss this issue later.

A useful tip

Before starting work on the paper, ask yourself, "Do I understand the assignment? What is the purpose of the writing? What am I trying to accomplish here? Do I know where to find facts and ideas for the paper? How much time do I want to spend on the paper and how much time do I have?" Asking these questions should help you to choose the most appropriate and relevant strategy.

Typically, a homework assignment will require you to do one or more of the following:

FACT FINDING. You must search for, locate, and demonstrate the facts or data requested in the assignment. Your job is to confirm a theory or an existing tendency. You do not have to argue about the suggested topic; your job is to demonstrate, prove, or disprove something. Examples: (1) Find some facts about the divorce rates in the United States. (2) Who were the most active voters in the United States in the 1990s: men or women?

DECISION MAKING. In this assignment, two or more options are already proposed. What you have to do is choose and defend one of the proposed alternatives. Examples: (1) Do you think it is possible to reduce the gap between the rich and the poor? (2) What is more important for an immigrant: (a) to get integrated into American culture, or (b) preserve his or her cultural identity, or (c) both?

PROBLEM SOLVING. Here you have to find your own answer to the question or problem introduced in the assignment. Unlike in decision making, you have to come up with your own theory, explanation, or idea. Therefore, you must support your answer with arguments. (You can use at least two strategies. First is the **inductive** method: you collect information and then offer your explanation. The **deductive** method is different: first you have an answer, a hypothesis; then you collect information in order to confirm that your answer is correct.) Examples: (1) Why are the crime rates higher in big cities than in small towns? (2) Choose a theory that—in your opinion—gives the most reasonable explanation of prejudice.

WRITTEN ASSIGNMENTS: BASIC ELEMENTS

Typically, unless the professor requires something else, your paper should contain several common elements. First, you have to write an introduction where you briefly describe the goal of your paper: a theory you defend, evidence you find, or an opinion that you want to express. It is fine to use a proverb or saying that reflects and conveys your main idea or point. Next, describe the method of your investigation (book review, newspaper review, Internet search, interviews you conducted yourself, and so on). Do not forget to identify and describe the sample: how many books or articles you reviewed, people you interviewed, websites you searched through, or television shows you watched. Then present your arguments in several paragraphs. Each paragraph should represent a particular idea, explanation of the idea, or description of somebody or something. Usually, the first sentence in the paragraph represents the main idea. The remainder of the paragraph expands on the idea. Example:

> **Researchers have identified considerable evidence that environment is related to the health status of individuals.** There are large national differences in life expectancy, but, in general, socioeconomic conditions and life expectancy are positively correlated. For instance, African Americans are three times as likely as Caucasians to be poor, and their life expectancy is six years short of Caucasians' life expectancy (U.S. National Center for Health Statistics, 1995). Illness and poverty are linked across countries. For example, although the overall AIDS-related death rate has declined,

the death rate for women continues to rise, particularly among those who are more likely to be poor compared to other groups (Cogan, 1997).

Finally, sum up your thoughts in a conclusion. State whether the goal described in the introduction was achieved. Sometimes it is a good idea to include your comments about how difficult or easy it was to work on the assignment, what new things you learned, and some new ideas you have about future research. In your conclusion, if it is appropriate, suggest where and how your data should be or could be used.

How and Where to Find Facts and Data

Your work on the paper should begin with the research for available literature and other sources of information.

- Search for books and journals. Besides the library at your college or university, you can visit any public library in your area, including county libraries. Most library services are free, except photocopying.
- Search for newspaper articles. Most newspapers have easily accessible websites where the most current reports are published. In addition, many libraries have software provided by major regional or national newspapers with articles published since the early 1990s.
- Search for databases on the Web. There are plenty of publicly available databases on the Internet. Your school may also have specialized databases accessible only through the school network. Consult with your library for instructions.
- Television. It is usually not the prime source of your research information, however, some fact finding can be done there. Major networks and local stations (see Chapter 9 on the media) have websites and usually publish transcripts of the most recent programming.

Interactive Reading

Reading the materials you have collected for the paper can be an interactive process. You might find some ideas that are useful and others not quite so. You might misunderstand one theory, and be inspired by another; you can agree or disagree with your findings. You can easily help yourself to remember any associations, ideas, and sometimes emotions that you experienced when you were reading the materials by preparing a set of symbols (see the box below).

Possible symbols:

!   This is a very important definition (description, theory, story, etc.)

?   I don't understand this. It needs further clarification.

Y   "Yes," I agree with the author; I have the same thoughts!

N   "No," I disagree with the author; I do not think he is right.

Q   "Question." I will have to ask my professor.

M   "More" information is needed. I would like to learn more about this topic or case.

Example:

Left Margin	Text (or notes)
Q	<u>Some . . . psychologists</u> studied the influence of birth order on the individual's behavior. The first child is almost always forced into second place by the birth of a little brother or sister. This might develop a sense of <u>inferiority</u> and protest against both the parents and the
?	new sibling. Alfred Adler wrote that the first born child finds himself deprived of the privileged position in the family after the birth of the sibling. The first-born becomes <u>resentful</u> and insecure. He may develop a
?	distrust of people and will try to secure his future against other sudden events in the future. The child becomes cautious and even <u>conservative</u> in his approach to life.
YM	

The symbols on the left margin indicate the following:

Q stands for a question you will ask about the names of psychologists who studied birth order and its influence on behavior: you couldn't hear the names and the professor didn't spell them.

? Two question marks indicate that there are two words (*inferiority* and *resentful*) you are not familiar with: you can guess their meanings but need exact translations. You will find them from your dictionary.

YM indicates that you agree with this statement ("Yes, it is true, I am more conservative and cautious than my younger brothers") and would like to learn more about the subject.

The easiest and most frequently used symbols are the exclamation point (!) and the question mark (?). The **"!"** almost always indicates that the sentence before it stands for something important, interesting, or meaningful. It identifies something you shouldn't miss when you start writing your paper. The **"?"** could indicate your misunderstanding of a concept. If you put it in front of a sentence, you could easily recognize that you should get additional information about this sentence. Many students might use only these two symbols. However, there could be other interactive marks. See the box on p. 91 for sample margin notations. You can write these symbols on the draft, printed copies of the materials you are working with, or in your notes. Please: **Never write on library books or journals.**

Thought Compression: How to Improve Understanding of Written Material

When you read a report from a newspaper and want to include some ideas from the report in your paper, it is important that you write down the most essential points of the article. This is done so that you can access the information more efficiently when the time comes to use it in your paper. In order to do this successfully, you have to learn how to generalize and categorize the information you are reading.

To convert a long paragraph into a shorter transcript, you have to recognize the most important points and the main ideas of the paragraph. Try to consolidate ideas: compress three, four, or five sentences into one.

Example 1 of thought compression:

Your political science professor says: "In 1992, Clinton was elected with 43 percent of the vote in a three-way election, and although analysts disagree on whether billionaire challenger Ross Perot cost Governor Clinton or President Bush more votes, there is little doubt that Clinton would still have won in a two-way race. You see, despite what some commentators say, the outcome should have been the same."

This is what might appear in your notes:

In 1992, Clinton won a three-man race with 42 percent of the votes, and perhaps, could have won in a two-man race.

Example 2 of thought compression:

Text suggests: Every person has his or her own theory according to which there is a balance between what one does and what one gets for it. We get angry when the balance is challenged by someone's actions. You get angry when you feel that you are entitled to get a promotion, but, instead, someone else gets promoted. You feel angry when the governor promised to lower your taxes, but ignores his promise four years later. Or, you get angry when you are waiting in a long line to buy a ticket and somebody sneaks into the line right in front of you.

This is what might appear in your notes:

We are angry when we feel entitled to something but do not obtain it: for instance, one sneaks into the line in front of you.

As many of our other skills, thought compression can be learned, practiced, and significantly improved. If you want to succeed at thought compression, then, read, listen, and practice.

Class exercises

Please convert each of the following paragraphs about prejudice into one sentence. Write the summary sentence after the paragraph. Hint: try to identify the main point or major idea of each paragraph.

1. Specialists argue about whether or not it is possible to overcome prejudice, whether or not it has always existed, and if it will continue to exist in human beings. Social scientists are divided on the issue: some remain optimistic, while others take a pessimistic view on prejudice and its origins. Let us briefly examine their arguments, both in defense of and against prejudice.

   _____

   _____

2. Pessimists argue that prejudice is a logical generalization based on facts and individual experiences. Well-educated and uneducated people could be equally prejudiced. Prejudice is a form of self-defense; if you get rid of it you disarm yourself. Equality is a sweet myth that is nice to place in political fairy tales. If social conditions outline the way you think, you will always be disappointed because somebody will always have more than you do, and there will always be somebody

   (continued)

Class exercises *(continued)*

who will try to get something from you. You will always protect what you have and blame those who frighten you.

_____

_____

3. The other group of pessimists suggests that prejudice is indeed an irrational fear. It is built into our psyche from the beginning of our lives. Aggression, violence, destruction, and humiliation have their deep roots in our unconscious mind. We can change the direction of aggression, but not aggression itself. Our thinking is schematic; therefore, we will always perceive this world as a continuous existence and struggle between opposites. Like day and night, hot and cold, men and women, good and evil, rich and poor—we will always think of the world in these categories. That is why we have both "friends" and "enemies" forever.

_____

_____

4. Optimists challenge pessimists by saying that prejudice is an irrational attitude based on ignorance and fear. When you open your mind, read, watch, listen, learn, educate yourself, and get rid of your irrational fears, you will reduce your prejudice. Cross-cultural interaction makes people less prejudiced. Interpersonal contacts, joint projects, international exchanges, and continuous communications all bring people closer to each other, make people friendlier to each other. Situations that are especially helpful are those in which people of different cultural backgrounds try to overcome obstacles together.

_____

_____

5. The optimists also say that social conditions direct your way of thinking. Whenever people become really equal, whenever they stop discriminating one group against another, the justification of prejudice will inevitably disappear. People compete for resources. If there is nothing to compete for, if nobody is left behind, then this will be the end of prejudice.

_____

_____

Homework assignments

Select a front-page article from a local newspaper. Read this article and, using three to four short sentences, write down the article's content. This exercise could be even more effective if you do it with a friend. After you finish, compare your notes. Refer back to the article and find out if you missed any important ideas and whether you interpreted them correctly.

You may choose a more difficult assignment if you have a VCR. Find a network that broadcasts the news. Push the recording button and begin taping the news. At the same time try to take notes and follow the fast-speaking news anchors. (You may skip the commercials.) After 10 minutes, stop recording and note taking. Rewind the tape and compare the videotaped news with your transcript. Note what important elements you missed. Try to analyze what was the most difficult for you to do. If you work on this assignment with a friend, compare your notes.

Spell or Misspell

When you write, do you always have to spell correctly, or can you take an easier approach and check the spelling later, when you have the time? Some people prefer to write everything correctly from the start. This accuracy helps them to be organized and precise. Other people feel better when they do not pay attention to the spelling because they want to be focused on what they write and do not want to forget their thoughts. They prefer to check the spelling later. Of course, you must check spelling before you submit your paper to your professor—no matter what subject it is. Some teachers may even deduct points off your grade because of spelling errors. In most cases, you can do a "spell check" on your computer. You can also ask your friend to check your paper for spelling errors. It is unnecessary for obvious misspellings to spoil the overall impression of your paper.

In English or . . . ?

Should you write the first draft in English or in your own language? Some students ask whether or not to use their native tongue when they write drafts (first versions) of papers, and then translate their work into English later. (In social science classes, for example, approximately 10% of students prefer to take notes in their native language; several class surveys conducted over three years in three schools in

A useful tip

You must have two copies of the assignment. Turn in the original and keep a copy for your files. Always include your name, course title, course number, and the date of the submission on the front page: it will help your professor with the grading.

Washington, D.C. and Virginia provided this evidence.) We would advise against this practice. First of all, this is not a wise investment of your time. It takes enormous intellectual effort to translate sentences from another language into English, and such translations are tiresome and often frustrating. Relying on translation also prohibits the full development of your English language skills. In addition, you may exhaust your psychological resources. Unless you are going to become a professional translator, try to prepare drafts and take notes in English.

A Few Words about Tape Recording

It is common to hear from students that they have difficulties writing a paper because they either do not like writing or they have too many thoughts, and it is difficult to organize them. In some cases—and, again, it can be helpful for some students but not so useful for others—you can use tape recording. Indeed, some students prefer to say or dictate their thoughts aloud, and then transcribe them into a text. What are the reasons for doing this? Some say it takes less time than to draft a paper. Others suggest that it is easier for them to say things

How to display references in your paper

For a book: indicate the author's name, year of publication, book title, city and state of publication, and publisher.

Example: Johnson, John. 1999. *How to Write Papers.* Boston, MA: New Publisher.

For an article: include the author's name, year of publication, article title, journal name, journal number, month of publication, and article pages.

Example: Robertson, Roberta & Bill Hope. 1998. On using references. *Journal of Modern References* 28, June, 45–50.

For a website: include the whole address of the site.

Example: http://references4u.com

than to write the same things down. Also, if you carry your voice recorder with you, then you can easily record a thought when it comes to you, no matter what you are doing at the time. Imagine trying to write something down while you are driving a car. That would be too dangerous. Using a voice recorder has some clear advantages over writing. Moreover, there are several inexpensive voice-converting softwares available today, and this technology is improving rapidly.

SIX RULES OF CRITICAL THINKING

Today you are a college student—an independent and free person. However, everyone knows that freedom goes side-by-side with responsibility. For example, we have to respect and obey both state and federal (national) laws. Moreover, the American Constitution establishes some fundamental principles of life that should be followed by everyone, no matter how long you have lived here, whether you stay permanently or temporarily. However, in the United States you are free to form your own ideas, ideals, and values. It naturally follows that if you are free to express your ideas, others are free to do the same, even if you dislike their views! Of course, being tolerant of other people's views is often difficult, and people often argue about the death penalty and abortion, they criticize presidents and local politicians, they have opposing ideas on how to reduce crime and whether or not the rich should help the poor. Sometimes people from other countries have a hard time understanding this reality and may feel confused by such a variety of opinions and beliefs. American culture has developed as a melting pot of ideas, values, and principles of living. To feel more comfortable within this whirlpool of opinions, one has to develop a strategy to examine, evaluate, and understand events, solve problems, and make decisions on the basis of evidence and reasoning, something that is commonly called critical thinking (Levy, 1997). If you understand and know how to apply some major principles of critical thinking to your written work, it will help you better understand evidence, interpret new facts, and defend your own ideas and beliefs.

Critical Thinking Rule No. 1: Know the Difference Between Facts and Opinions

When students solve a math problem, it is expected that they will all get the same result. This is because, in most cases, there is one, and only one, correct answer for the math problem. $2 \times 2 = 4$ for all people, in every country. However, when you write a paper for sociology, history, psychology, or another social science class, in most cases, there are no "correct" answers. What professors evaluate in your work is strength of your arguments, in other words, how well they defend your opinions. Why is it important to know the distinction between opinions and facts?

There is a view held by many that descriptions of what we see or hear can never be entirely objective or neutral. People bring into descriptions their personal feelings and values. The words people use not only describe things and events around them, but can evaluate

A class assignment

Consider the following statements. Identify (a) facts and (b) opinions. Explain your choices.

In the United States, homosexuality is considered to be a mental disorder. However, despite many people's objections, this type of sexual behavior is openly discussed in the media.

Homosexuality was considered a disorder prior to 1972. Today, it is not a mental disorder, according to the American Psychiatric Association's classification of mental disorders. So the first sentence is an incorrect statement. The second sentence is a fact. Why? Because, indeed, we know through observation that many people have strong negative opinions against homosexuality, and homosexuality is openly discussed in the media.

Americans believe that it is more important to protect the rights of those accused of crimes than to be tough on criminals.

If this statement reflects someone's opinion, there is no problem. However, if someone suggests that this statement is a fact, this person will be wrong. In 1998, 76 percent of Americans surveyed believed that it was more important to be tough on criminals, and only 17 percent thought about protecting their rights (2 percent were undecided). (WP/Kaizer Foundation/Harvard University Survey; August 10–27, 1998).

In the United States in a single day, the number of people who are getting married is only twice as big as the number of people who are getting divorced.

This statement represents a general fact known to sociologists: in any given day, there are approximately as many marriages as divorces taking place.

these things and events. Therefore, in your research papers, unless this is what the professor asks you to do, avoid presenting your value judgments as objective reflections of truth. If you express your opinion, it should be supported by facts that can be verifiable by other people. Facts improve the strength of your argument.

Do not let anyone say to you that you cannot express your opinions. You can express yourself in many ways, and the law protects your right to free speech. But you have to call your opinions and not confuse them with facts. For example, if you find data indicating that just 50 percent of eligible voters in the United States actually vote in presidential elections, this is a fact. Why? Because the published data shows how many people voted in the United States at that time. However, when you try to explain this fact, you now express your opinion. You may say, for example, that voter apathy and disappointment in politics caused this relatively low voting turnout. This is your opinion because you do not know why the level is low. You are just guessing. Another person may suggest a different explanation: "The number of voters is low because of people's satisfaction with life. Things are going fine and it does not really matter who is in power. The government plays a very small role in people's lives and either candidate will be fine in office."

Facts are supposed to be neutral. Opinions reflect what you think or feel about the facts. It was a fact in 1998 that almost nine out of ten American parents surveyed did not want or would not want their adult children to live with them (Strong, et al., 1998). You are expressing an opinion when you attempt to explain the fact presented in the previous sentence. You may say that young Americans can afford to live alone; therefore, there is no harm for them to leave home at age 18. You may also suggest that the ties between parents and children are not as strong as those in many other cultures.

Another example would be to imagine that a group of armed men captured hostages in some countries. Many people would call these men terrorists. However, some people might call them freedom fighters. The hostage-taking incident has taken place; this is the fact. Our interpretations of the event may be different. Dictators can be described as

> ## Useful tips
>
> Pay attention to whether your paper expresses an opinion or a fact. When you know that you can confirm your statements with available facts, use them, or at least mention their existence. In other cases, do not hesitate to use such phrases as "in my opinion," "I think," "I believe," "it seems to me," "according to my views," and so on.

"strong leaders"; and bribery may be referred to as "gratitude." By observing how other people describe things, we can learn a lot about these people.

Remember to consider the source of the information. Inaccurate results cannot be proven, or there is a great deal of doubt about their validity. Opinions are always subjective and even if they are based on facts, they reflect the viewpoint of the person who holds the opinion.

Critical Thinking Rule No. 2: There Are Many Colors in a Rainbow

Many things in life are certain, and we can say "yes" or "no" when we describe them. For example, you passed an exam and got an "A." It would be untrue to say that you got a "B." You arrive at the airport and realize that you are late for your flight and the plane has already taken off. You missed your plane. You are not on the plane because you are standing at the airport terminal trying to schedule another flight. If you are born in Korea, your birthplace is not Paris or Lima. These things are obvious, you say. Facts are always facts! Do not be so certain, however. There are many facts people misinterpret every day! We may say, for example, that Mister Ababaka is unkind and mean because, at times, Mr. Ababaka was unkind to us. Conclusion? He is a mean person. However, do we have evidence that he has *never* been kind to others? If we do not have such evidence, we can only conclude that Mr. Ababaka was mean in the observable instances.

Most psychological categories and descriptions we ascribe to people and their behavior do not consider all the factors involved. People say often: a violent person, a very happy student, an indecisive individual, or an undisciplined child. Do these descriptions reflect the real situation or tell us a lot about these people? Probably not. What is the level of the person's violence? Is he dangerous or not? How do we define *happy*? How often does he show indecisiveness? Does this suggest that when one uses critical thinking there is no right or wrong in life? We do not think so. There is right and wrong behavior, and right and wrong decisions. There are universal moral values shared by the vast majority of people on earth. However, there are many aspects of our behavior that we evaluate from the standpoint of our traditions, values not shared by other groups. For example, among Americans, a majority (55 percent) believe that there should be clear community standards for right and wrong. However, as many as 35 percent of Americans disagree and believe that every individual should live by her or his own moral standards (WP/Kaizer Foundation/Harvard University Survey; August 10–27, 1998).

People tend to categorize things, including other people. We put into categories everything from persons to places, from events to feelings. When we categorize, we often unintentionally assume that all people who belong to this category have a particular characteristic or can be described in the same way. We often say that men display aggressive behavior more often than women do, that children of middle-class parents get better grades at school as compared to children of poor parents, that Asian–Americans have higher scores on intelligence tests than other ethnic groups in the United States. Such categorization is also called stereotyping (for more information and interactive exercises see Chapter 8 on stereotyping). Stereotypes sometimes do not allow us to see facts critically. Let's take a look at the previous examples. There can be women who are more aggressive than men; there are children of poor parents who have the highest grades; and there are millions of people representing every ethnic group whose intelligence scores are higher than average. Even if you consider yourself to be an open-minded person, do not underestimate the extent to which your categorizations can affect your current experience, impressions, and perceptions.

When describing someone, try to make your statements specific rather than applicable to all other people or groups. For example, we might say about someone: "She has both a pleasant and an ugly side to her character." This can be said about almost anyone on earth. Or, consider this statement: "Americans want to be happy." It would be interesting to know if are there any nations whose people do not want to be happy. Someone writes: "Italians are hospitable people." "Does a nation exist where all people are not hospitable at all?" These statements fail to reveal anything distinctive about a given person or social group because they are valid about all people in general.

Critical thinking is about making comparisons. We often say, "These two religions are so different" or "These two ethnic groups are similar to each other." However, there is nothing that can be perfectly identical or entirely different from other things. Finding the similarities and differences between

---

Useful tips

To improve the strength of your argument, use such words as: "most of the time," "in many situations," "predominantly," "a majority of," "in general." If you describe a fact or behavior, describe under what circumstances this behavior occurs or the fact takes place.

Think critically

When comparing and contrasting something, describe in what ways these things are similar and in what ways they are different. Choose different standpoints from which you will evaluate. Despite what may appear to be an overwhelming number of similarities between two events, always search for and take into account their differences. Conversely, regardless of what may seem to be a total absence of commonalities between two events, search for and take into account their similarities.

Assignment: Despite obvious differences, find and describe similarities between:

Republicans and Democrats; New York and Los Angeles; American food and Chinese food; rock music and hip-hop; Ford and General Motors; New York Yankees and Boston Red Sox; Tommy Hillfiger and Nike; public schools and private schools.

something is based on the perspective from which you choose to view them. In this way, most people and events can be seen as both distinct from and, at the same time, similar to other events or people.

Critical Thinking Rule No. 3: Emotions Should Not Judge Facts!

In the classic TV series *Star Trek*, there is a main character, Mr. Spock, who is half-human, half-alien, and is naturally free from any emotions. His behavior is directed by pure logic. He is, of course, a fictional character; all humans experience emotions. A strong emotional commitment to something or somebody is a natural element of human life. However, people's personal likes and dislikes sometimes tell more about the individuals themselves than about the objects under their consideration.

Consider the following statements:

"I dislike individuals with liberal views. I think everything they do is an attempt to raise taxes on hard-working Americans."

"I dislike men and women with conservative views and believe that they are narrow-minded and greedy. The only thing they care about is their wallet."

"I love this actor (Jim Carey, Julia Roberts, Helen Hunt, Jack Nicholson), and will buy tickets to see his/her recent premier regardless of what people say about the movie."

"I do not like this actor (Jim Carey, Julia Roberts, Helen Hunt, Jack Nicholson), and will not see his/her recent movie."

"I think that most immigrants to the United States are poor, uneducated, and unskilled individuals who arrive in the country illegally. Therefore, immigration should be restricted."

"I think that most immigrants to the United States are educated and hard-working individuals who arrive in the country in search of a new life. Therefore, immigration should be encouraged and protected."

Every statement here begins with an evaluation of a particular group. The positive or negative evaluation then results in a suggested action in support of or against the considered people. Our emotions dictate further actions. People often do not have the time or resources to consider all information available to them. Instead, they use emotions to make judgments. We all have a repertoire of such shortcuts that we tend to use automatically, without necessarily considering their accuracy or validity in various life situations. Thus, we may either like or dislike particular groups of people or individuals because of their nationality, religion, sexual or political orientation.

Vivid examples, dramatic events, graphic case studies, and personal testimonies, in contrast to statistical information are likely to exert a disproportionate impact on our judgments. In this way, anecdotes and stories may be more persuasive than factual data. For example, look at any evening news broadcast. Perhaps you are disturbed. You find the local news filled with reports about accidents, theft, robbery, assault, and other violent crime. Persuaded by the intimidating power of the evening news, one may conclude that violent crime is on the rise in this country. In fact, quite the opposite trend has occurred since the middle of the 1990s. Another example is that many tourists and visitors say they are surprised how divided America is on the abortion issue. Politicians, radio and television commentators, newspapers and magazines frequently cover this debate. Consequently, abortion appears to be a major political issue in this country that seriously affects election results. In fact, statistical data does not prove that. Public opinion polls show that only a very small percentage of Americans—up to 10 percent—consider abortion an important issue that affects their voting behavior (Andersen, 1997).

> ### *A useful tip*
>
> When you work on a paper, keep an open mind to different and, especially, challenging points of view. Do not cling to your emotional judgments, particularly in the face of evidence to the contrary.

Sometimes single facts may cause various emotions or speedy assessments. A more detailed analysis may suggest different interpretations. Sixteen percent of Americans lived without health insurance in the late 1990s, compared to 14 percent in 1990. The number of people below poverty level increased by 1997 to 35.6 million people, almost 2 million higher than in 1990! These numbers could suggest that the U.S. economy did not do very well during the 1990s. However, during the same period, the unemployment rate fell to 4.5 percent (a 1 percent drop since 1990), and the median family income rose from $35,000 to more than $44,000 since 1990.

A useful tip

Be empathetic, i.e., try to understand something you do not like from the position of people who disagree with you. Although emotional and vivid events may be very persuasive, they do not necessarily tell us about general tendencies. Make an effort, whenever it is reasonable, to look for statistical information about the event you are examining. When faced with a discrepancy between your beliefs and the facts, resist the natural tendency to assume that your beliefs are right and the facts are wrong.

One very important way in which our personal views can bias (prejudice) our thinking is when we equate our description of "what is" with our prescription of "what ought to be." This occurs, for instance, whenever we define what is good in terms of what is "typical." Learn to differentiate objective descriptions from subjective prescriptions. Don't make the mistake of equating statistical frequency with moral value. Thus, if most people do something, that does not make it intrinsically right; if most people do not, neither does it make it wrong. In like manner, if most people do something, that does not make it wrong; if they do not, that does not make it right (Levy, 1997).

Critical Thinking Rule No. 4: Naming Something is Not Explaining It

In an effort to find an explanation for events or issues, sometimes people commit the following error. Imagine, for instance, that you have to write a paper about aggressive driving on American roads. You seek to explain why many people ignore speed signs, do not use their turn signal, and drive recklessly. You find several newspaper articles on this issue and believe you have found the correct explanation, one that is suggested by the newspaper reporters also. You establish that the main reason for aggressive driving is people's disregard for the rights of other drivers: some people do not care about other human beings and are willing to put them in dangerous situations. Be cautious, however. Does this sentence actually explain the nature of aggressive driving? No, it does not. Why? Because the explanation is redundant. Aggressive driving by definition is, in fact, the disregard for other people's rights on the road. What you set out to do is explain why some people act carelessly. Perhaps you will conclude that several psychological reasons play a role, such as emotional problems that some individuals have, an inability to stay on schedule, frustrating events of the day, or maybe some other reasons.

> ### A useful tip
>
> Remember: by giving an event a different name you are not explaining this event. When looking for an explanation to something, ask yourself a question: does my description add anything to my understanding of this problem?

Let's take another example. You realize that there are some people in the United States who donate money to charitable organizations. Why do they do this? You may answer: they do it because they like to help other people. This answer makes sense, of course, but does it add anything new to our understanding of generous behavior? Not really, because it is obvious that if a person does not like to help other people then she will not donate money to charity. To answer this question from a critical thinking standpoint, you will have to look for several explanations. Some people do charitable work because their religion suggests that they do it. Others give money to charity because they want to get a tax break. Others do it because they were poor themselves and know how nice it is to get support from other people.

A topic to think about

Consider another interesting case. It was found, for example, that in the *New York Times,* a leading American newspaper, that there are more stories published about homeless people during winter than summer. Some experts say this is because more readers pay more attention to such stories during the holiday season, which starts in November and ends in January (Bunis, et al., 1996). This explanation appears to be plausible. However, it does not go far enough. Indeed, why do people pay more attention to such stories? Perhaps because they feel how cold it is outside. Or, because they have learned since childhood that the holiday season is the time for sharing. Or, maybe newspaper editors send their reporters on assignments to write about the homeless because it is considered politically correct to express compassion to others during the holiday season. Do you have your own suggestions about this case?

Some may send money to charity in order to be in line with his friends who have already contributed.

As an exercise, find some flaws of reasoning in the following statements:

Some people express prejudice against other ethnic groups because these people are racists.

A man sells his property because he wants to earn some money.

The couple is getting a divorce because husband and wife cannot live together.

Critical Thinking Rule No. 5: A Link Between Two Events Does Not Indicate that One Event Is Causing the Other One

Let us begin with an example. It is known that children who are prone to violent behavior tend to watch television programs with violent content more often than nonviolent children do. The most obvious explanation that comes to us might be that watching violent television programs may cause violent behavior in individuals. However, one has to take a more careful look at the problem of violence and television. A different explanation can be offered: what if children with violent tendencies prefer to watch television programs with violent content? Indeed, research indicates that the relationship between aggressive behavior and watching television violence is two-directional. That is, aggressive children are prone to watch violent TV programs, and television violence, in turn, results in aggressive behavior.

A class exercise

Consider the links between human creativity and mood disorders. Psychologists have concluded that among creative people, e.g., musicians, poets, and artists, mood disorders are more common than they are in other peoples (see Jamison, 1993). What two types of connection can you establish? What causes what? Do mood disorders affect creativity, or does creativity affect mood disorders?

Let us consider another sociological fact. In the United States and around the world, crime rates in poor neighborhoods are higher than the crime rates in other, more affluent communities. The simple answer is that poverty causes crime. Is this a wrong assumption? No, it can be a correct one, however, why don't we look at another option? Crime, in turn, may contribute to poverty as well. Because crime-infested areas do not attract private business to invest in these sections, tourists stay away from these neighborhoods, and as a result, new jobs are not created and local residents have fewer opportunities to earn money.

What you see as cause may be seen as effect and vice versa. Many people's answers to cause-and-effect dilemma are based on their personal views. Don't assume before thinking about something seriously that a link between two events is a "one-way street." Every possibility might be both cause and effect on the other. Remember the chicken-and-egg question: which came first? Quite often, questions of this type are difficult and sometimes unnecessary to answer.

When we judge other people, we have a tendency to explain their behavior in context of their own personality. At the same time, we often minimize (or even ignore) the importance of the particular context or situation. For example, imagine a person you know who does not say hello to you in passing. The person, then, is rude. Or isn't he? Maybe he did not see you, or he was extremely preoccupied with his own thoughts. Maybe you didn't say hello loud enough. If somebody doesn't want to lend you his notes, you consider this person to be inconsiderate. You do not know that maybe this person has already promised to give his notes to somebody else, or maybe is planning to study them at home. American journalists know this tendency of human judgment. Research shows that television viewers tend to interpret reports about the "real" homeless, jobless, or poor individuals in a specific way: many consider that these people's problems are caused by themselves (i.e., they are lazy, unmotivated, etc.) and not by the society. The viewers' attitudes change when the reporter pays more attention to abstract facts and figures on the state or national levels. In these cases, people will tend to think more about societal causes of poverty and homelessness.

Critical Thinking Rule No. 6: When You Explain Why Certain Things Happen, Think about Many Causes

Imagine that your friend got involved in a fender-bender (a minor car accident): she bumped into another car near an intersection. When you ask your friend to explain what happened, she says that the girl in a car in front of her suddenly stopped on a yellow light, and as a result of this "sudden" stop your friend did not have enough time to react properly and push the brakes. "So, who caused the accident?" you ask. "The car ahead of me," your friend replies. Did it? When you ask your friend to tell you more abut her day, you realize that to begin with, she was at a birthday party the night before and came home late. Because she went to bed very late, she overslept in the morning. Because she was in a hurry to get to school, she jumped into her car and forgot to take her purse, so she had to make a u-turn and go back home, which took her another 20 minutes. Her frustration grew because of the traffic on the main street. In order to beat the traffic and be at school on time, she decided to take a shortcut. Then she got lost. Because she was desperately late, she started to drive very fast and ignore speed limits. As a result, she got involved in an accident.

Now try to answer the question: what was the cause of the accident? Was it a car that stopped at the intersection? Or was it your friend's decision to stay late at that party? Or was it because she overslept and left her bag in her apartment? Or maybe heavy traffic on the main street was to blame? Now you can predict the direction of this reasoning: from a critical thinking standpoint, all of the above circumstances could have contributed to the collision.

Let us use another example. Florida, a state in the southeastern United States, has the highest proportion of population (18.5 percent) over age 65. On the other hand, Alaska has the lowest rank of people over 65 at 5.3 percent of the population. Could you offer an explanation for this trend? Some may quickly suggest that the answer is the climate. Alaska has the harshest climate in the United States, whereas Florida is known for its warm weather. However, weather could be a poor predictor of why American senior citizens choose a particular state in which to live. Pennsylvania and Rhode Island, two states that come second and third with almost 16 percent of senior population, have climates quite different from Florida's and winter in both these states can

For class discussion

The states with the highest proportion of population under 18 are Utah (33%), Alaska (31%), and Idaho (29%), all three with relatively harsh climates. Can you explain this tendency as climate-related? What other factors may cause a high level of young people in a state?

The top five states with the highest proportion of doctors (more than 300 per 100,000 population) are all in the northeastern part of the United States: Massachusetts, New York, Maryland, Connecticut, and Rhode Island. Do you think that doctors like the weather conditions of these regions? What other factors may affect a doctor's decision to live in a particular state?

be severe. The answer may be that there is no single answer regarding why some individuals choose a particular place to live. For some people it could be climate (cold or warm), for others it could be low property taxes. Some people move closer to their children and grandchildren. Some want to go back to their hometowns.

Take a look at some more examples. What triggers the development of mental disorders? Is it genetic or biological factors? Unfavorable social conditions? Continuing stress? Persistent abuse? The answer is: all of the above conditions may contribute (Levy, 1997). What causes almost one million people to apply for American citizenship every year? Is this motivated by their desire to escape injustice and war in their home countries? Maybe these people are in search of a better life in the United States. Maybe America offers greater educational opportunities for children. Or maybe this decision is based on a desire to reunite with relatives. Apparently, all the above reasons can be true (Shiraev, et al., 2000). What causes violent behavior in some individuals? Is it long-term abuse and injustice they have suffered, or a short temper that is quick to anger? Apparently both (Tsytsarev & Grodnitzky, 1995).

It is known that wealthier people live longer and are generally healthier than poorer people. Why is this? One obvious reason is that wealthier people can afford more medical care than the less fortunate. However, other factors contribute to this trend. For example, people with higher income smoke less, exercise more, maintain healthy body weight, eat nutritious meals, and face less psychological stress than other groups (*Mental Medicine*, 1994).

In 1998, Americans charged 40 percent more on their credit cards ($1,308 billion) than they did in 1990 ($796 billion). Does it mean that

A useful tip

In attempting to explain why an event occurred, don't limit your search to one cause. Instead, explore multiple plausible causes, all of which may be responsible for producing the effect. When faced with an either/or question, always consider the possibility that the answer might be both.

For class discussion

Try to find multiple causes/explanations to the following questions:

In your opinion, why are divorce rates higher in the United States than they are in Kuwait? In your opinion, why are crime rates in American cities higher than those in urban areas? In your opinion, why is the American female soccer team among the best in the world, whereas the American men have had poor performance in international soccer championships? Why is *Baywatch* among the most popular television shows in the world?

Americans are spending more than they did in the early 1990s? This may be true. However, it may be that Americans simply have started to use credit cards more often than they did ten years ago. Today, most small businesses will accept your credit card, which was not the case in previous decades. If it is convenient and people like this payment system, they are more willing to use "plastic" instead of cash or checks.

DETAILS, DETAILS . . .

A word about your writing style. What is the appropriate style for a given paper, formal or informal? A paper written informally resembles a conversation. Such a paper conveys certain emotions, for example, joy, frustration, surprise. It may be sarcastic or humorous. A formal style is more neutral in terms of the emotions conveyed. Formal papers contain no slang; informal write-ups, on the contrary, allow the usage of slang. For example, using the formal style, you always describe a person as a man or woman, lady or gentleman, human being or person. Adopting the informal style, one can address another person as dude, guy, bro, or pal. Under no circumstances would it be appropriate to use profanity in your reports. According to traditions of higher education, it is always expected that the writer find other, more appropriate words to describe people's actions and personalities. No matter what style you choose, refer to yourself as "I," or use the slightly more formal "we." Pay attention to gender-related words as some readers could be sensitive to gender bias in your report. Remember, there are congressmen and congresswomen; it is appropriate to write "chairwoman" and "spokeswoman." If you do not know how to reflect gender in someone's title, learn how to use other, gender-neutral words, such as firefighter (both a man and a woman can be a firefighter), cop, office, chair, specialist, and so on.

You would be surprised how small things can spoil the overall quality of your paper. Therefore, when the paper or report is finished, check to see if you took care of all the "minor" details that can affect your grade. Be sure to submit a title page with the paper if the professor has required students to do so. If you use references, do not forget to include the reference list, even though it may contain only a few items. Unless otherwise requested by the professor, always staple the pages of the paper together. Leave 2 to 2.5-inch margins so that the professor can write her comments on them. Use 1.5 or 2-line spacing. Always have a second copy of your work and keep it with your class materials. Submit your paper on time (see the box below). Organize your time. Review your paper and let it rest. Use proofreaders.

> ### *A topic to think about*
>
> Following are some excuses that students still use and almost every college professor has already heard at least several times. Therefore, do not use them because your professor is likely to offer a powerful argument in response:
>
> - My computer's hard drive crashed yesterday. My brother (sister, nephew, cousin, dog, cat, etc.) accidentally deleted my file. **Response:** Have a copy of your work on a removable diskette.
> - My printer is out of ink and my printer's cartridge is out of powder. **Response:** Do your printing job at any of the school's printers.
> - I had two (three, four, etc.) tests this week, so I need an extension. Or: Professor, I was thinking a lot about the assignment and finally realized that I do not quite understand the assignment. **Response:** Do your work in advance; you knew about this assignment long ago.
> - I couldn't open my file on the school's computer. May I bring the paper tomorrow? **Response:** Try to open the file at least a day before your paper is due. Ask the computer lab staff to help you.
> - Professor, here is my diskette (waving one). I have just a few final touches to make; let me bring the paper later. **Response:** Do not think that you are smarter than your professor and that just seeing the disk will impress him. Bring your paper instead.

AVOID PLAGIARISM

Sometimes you browse the Internet or look through a pile of books in the library and find the perfect material for your report or paper. The site offers almost everything you need: a great introduction, a literature review, solid empirical data, critical analysis of the data, a spectacular conclusion, and even a bibliography! While contemplating an inevitable "A," you copy this material from the website (or scan it) and paste into your file. You change the fonts, the design of the report, put your name on the top, and submit it to your professor. What you have done is called **plagiarism,** or the intentional use of someone else's ideas as your own. Plagiarism is cheating and can be severely penalized (you can fail the class and be expelled from college). In some cases you can be charged with a violation of copyright laws, and the consequences of this action can be very serious. Remem-

A useful tip

If you want to avoid plagiarism, mention the author whose work you are using as many times as necessary. There is nothing wrong in promoting other people's ideas and giving them credit for their work. Use quotation marks if you want to cite an entire sentence or two. However, do not make the citations too frequent and too long.

ber, you have to submit your own ideas. If you base your report on ideas of other people, you must include their names and mention their publications. Do not think you can "trick" your professor by changing the introduction and conclusion, leaving the middle part intact. Your paper is still plagiarized. Do not try to substitute 10, 15, or 20 words from the original text as your own. It will still be unacceptable. Neither can you submit one paper to several professors for different classes. Likewise, you cannot use a paper written by another student and claim that it is yours. Remember, one silly mistake may influence your entire college career.

Part Three

Negotiating American Culture

Part One of this book covered many of the difficult and confusing technical details that students need to understand in order to comfortably and successfully arrive in the United States and begin studying. Chapter 3 dealt with the concept of "culture shock" and what happens when the culture you bring as an international student interacts with the cultural realities of a new school that exists in a new community, in a new state, in a new country. Part Two covered some important skills and strategies to help you understand what is expected of you in the classroom and in your coursework. Most of the issues in Part One and Part Two relate to both significant and subtle institutional differences that you will immediately encounter upon arrival and as you begin to negotiate the college and community in which you have selected to study and live. Not knowing about these issues can cause confusion and make adjusting to life in your new setting difficult.

It is important for you to understand and be prepared to deal with a new setting that will be different from and may not operate the way you are used to and the way that you like best. Your goal will be to develop ways in which you can recognize and adapt to new situations that you may or may not fully understand. Part Three of this book covers aspects of the culture in the United States that will help you to *begin* to understand the sometimes confusing and frequently misunderstood concept of American culture.

Chapter 6

Culture

You have turned on your television set and tuned into a late-night show that features several people who are laughing, talking, and sometimes even arguing with each other. They are talking about schools and money. Frequently during the discussion, the names of the discussants are displayed for a few seconds. You try to catch the names, one by one: Coolio, Oprah, G. Gordon Liddy, and Bill Maher. Who are these people? They represent different facets of American contemporary culture: music, television, politics, and radio. Are you familiar with any of these individuals? If not, don't be disappointed: not every American can identify all these names. However, you will be able to identify them. This, in fact, will be our next assignment: Just type these names in the search box of any Web search engine and wait for the results.

I t is very complicated to begin a dialog about culture in the United States. At first glance, one might think that there isn't any clear culture at all and that it is a society of fragmented and competing groups of people. However, this is not the case.

The United States has a heterogeneous population. This means that it is made up of many different groups that make this country diverse and multicultural. Americans have a cultural identity that has many dimensions and is described as being *pluralistic*. This is particularly true in urban areas, but is becoming more of a reality in suburban and rural areas, as well.

DEFINING CULTURE

The *American Heritage Dictionary* defines **culture** as "The totality of socially transmitted behavior patterns characteristic of a people." What does that mean? A way to clarify this definition is to focus on what the phrase "totality of socially transmitted behavior patterns" represents. Stern (1992) and Maley (1993) do a good job of breaking down the idea of culture to six aspects:

Six Aspects of Culture

Places. This has to do with geography: Local and regional variation.

History. The objective set of facts and events that shaped a region and the perceptions and beliefs people have about their own history.

Individual persons. How people live, what they think, do, and value.

People in society. The way in which a society functions and how economic, professional, age, sex, ethnic, and religious groups interact in it.

Institutions. The influence of the democratic system of government and how the bureaucracy, education, social welfare, the law, and the media interact.

Art, music, literature, sports, and other major achievements.

A useful tip

The generalizations in the chart barely touch upon the natural beauty of the United States. Most states have a webpage that provides a great deal of information and statistics. You can find the World Wide Web address by typing

http://www.state.(*postal abbreviation*).us

Each state is identified by two characters: **CA** stands for California, **NY** for New York, **OR** for Oregon, **TX** for Texas, **NC** for North Carolina, and so on. For example, for California you would type **http://www.state.ca.us** and for Virginia you would type **http://www.state.va.us.**

PLACES

In Chapter 1, you were advised to carefully select the school that you plan to attend based on your program of study and the area of the country in which you are interested. There is a great deal of geographic variation in the U.S. and that variation can potentially have an immense impact on the quality of your stay. You should fully understand not only the geography of the area in which you plan to study, but also any cultural characteristics of that area. The *conterminous states** can be divided into regions that reflect common characteristics; however, each state has its own personality and charm, as described in the chart below. Hawaii and Alaska are strongly influenced by their unique and beautiful geography and by their detachment from the conterminous states. Canada separates Alaska from the mainland and Hawaii is in the Pacific Ocean.

---

*The conterminous states are those states that share a border with another state, thus forming the major body of the United States.

Region	States in the Region	Regional Character
New England	Maine, New Hampshire, Vermont, Massachusetts, Rhode Island, Connecticut	Rocky, wooded mountain and valley areas, picturesque seaports and rocky coastlines, with a great deal of natural beauty. Mild summer, fall, and spring seasons with very cold winters.
Middle Atlantic	New York, New Jersey, Pennsylvania, Delaware, Maryland, Washington, D.C., Virginia	Rolling hills, wooded areas, and low- to medium-sized mountain ranges. Lush, green valleys with moderate vegetation. Very good farmlands. Highly developed coastal areas. Cold winters and hot summer seasons, with mild fall and spring seasons.
The South	Georgia, North Carolina, South Carolina, Kentucky, West Virginia, Florida, Alabama, Mississippi, Louisiana, Arkansas, Tennessee	Rolling, wooded areas with low- to medium-sized mountain areas. Much more vegetation than in the Middle Atlantic and it is sub-tropic to tropic in the deep south. Many rivers and lakes run through the South. Farming is good. Mild winter, fall, and spring seasons, with very hot and humid summers.
The Plains	North Dakota, South Dakota, Nebraska, Kansas	Very large areas of flat, grassy land in Kansas and Nebraska, more rocky and mountainous in the Dakotas. This area tends to be dry and has very harsh winters, with mild spring, fall, and summer seasons. Farming and raising livestock are good in this region.
The Midwest	Ohio, Indiana, Illinois, Michigan, Wisconsin, Minnesota, Iowa, Missouri	This region is characterized by the Great Lakes and the other lakes and rivers that run throughout the region, including the Mississippi River. This region has mountains and wooded areas, as well as rolling flatlands, and is excellent for farming and livestock. Mild summer, fall, and spring seasons, and very harsh winters.

(continued)

(Continued)

Region	States in the Region	Regional Character
The Southwest	Oklahoma, Texas, Arizona, New Mexico, Nevada, Utah, Colorado, and Southern California	These states all have relatively dry climates that are either desert-like or extremely mountainous. The desert areas are very hot in the summer season with mild winter, fall, and spring seasons. The northern areas of Arizona, New Mexico, Colorado, and Utah can have severe winters, with heavy snowfall. This region has breathtaking canyon regions, as well.
The Northwest	Oregon, Washington, Idaho, Montana, Wyoming, and Northern California	Great mountainous, wooded areas with rocky coastlines are characteristic of this region. This region is full of natural beauty, and is not highly populated. Mild summer, fall, and spring seasons with relatively cold winters.

HISTORY AND DEMOCRATIC GOVERNMENT

We could not possibly cover the details of the history of the development of the United States in this text. However, it is important to note some significant historical issues that relate to culture. Like all countries in the world, the culture of this country has been strongly influenced by its historic developments. Even though the United States is a relatively young country compared to others, it has had a rich history and has risen in a short time to be a great and powerful nation.

From the settlement of Jamestown, Virginia, in 1620 to the present, people have been coming to this country to begin a new life in which they are in control of their personal lives. This is reflected in the documents that serve as the basis of democracy in the U.S.: The Declaration of Independence and the Constitution.

The Declaration of Independence served in 1776 to give notice to the ruling colonial government from Great Britain that "these united colonies [America] are, and of right ought to be, free and independent states." Thomas Jefferson, the principle author of the document, stated that:

"All men are created equal" and "are endowed by their creator with certain unalienable rights, including life, liberty, and the pursuit of happiness."

—"To secure these rights, governments are instituted [started] among men, deriving their just powers from the consent of the governed."

—"Whenever any form of government becomes destructive of these ends, it is the right of the people to alter or to abolish it, and to institute a new government." (Cit. from I. Gordon, 1981)

The Constitution of the U.S.A. was ratified by the thirteen colonies in 1789. It served as the blueprint of the U.S. government and established the initial laws of the land. The Constitution is comprised of Articles I–VIII (one through eight), which established the structure of the democratic form of government in the U.S., insuring the balance of power between the executive, judicial, and legislative units. The executive branch is represented by the President, the Vice-president, and the Cabinet, which consists of the heads of the executive departments, and the support staff that help the President run his end of the government. (We are using the masculine pronouns "he" and "his" to refer to the President because there has not been a female President yet, although there might be one in the future.) The executive branch is often referred to as "The White House" in the media; however, the executive branch has offices in many other places. The President and his family live in "The White House," which has offices for the President and his large staff.

The main function of the executive branch is to provide leadership for the federal government and to represent the United States abroad. The president's role of running the government is in direct relation to the other branches of government. The President is not all-powerful. Both the judicial and the legislative branches temper his power. On top of this, he must ultimately answer to the people.

The legislative branch of the government is comprised of the House of Representatives and the Senate. The Senate and the House make up what is referred to as *Congress*. The legislative branch has always had "the power of the purse." The control of the budget of the U.S. government is a powerful check on the executive branch. The Senate consists of 100 members: two senators from each state, who serve six-year terms. Currently, the House consists of 435 voting members that represent the states based on the size of the population, and each member serves two-year terms. The House and the Senate work on originating "bills" that set policy and appropriate money for the operation of the federal government; they also set policy for how many governmental agencies should operate. Bills are proposed legislation that must pass through the House and the Senate and are ultimately signed into law by the President. The President's check on the legislative branch is that he has the power to sign or veto (reject) a bill from Congress. Congress creates legislation; the President signs legislation into law; and the judicial branch of the government interprets and makes rulings based on law.

The judicial branch of the government is represented by the federal court system, which is comprised of the Supreme Court, and the circuit and district court systems. The circuit court system and the district court system handle most of the federal cases. The Supreme Court is the judicial body that makes final interpretation of law, a sort of guardian of the Constitution.

The Constitution also has XXVII (27) amendments that add to the content of the original articles. The first 10 amendments are known as the "Bill of Rights" and were ratified in order to protect individual freedom from the tyranny of government. The Constitution has been preserved, and has very carefully been amended to meet the changes in our development as a nation. For detailed information about our system of government, set your Web browser to http://thomas.loc.gov.

One of the fundamental principles of the United States is the importance of the freedom of the individual person. The *"Founding Fathers"* were careful to make this very clear from the inception of the country. The idea of individual freedom is strongly represented in the two primary documents that we mentioned earlier: The Declaration of Independence and the Constitution of the U.S. government (particularly through the "Bill of Rights").

Rights Enumerated in the Bill of Rights[*]

First Amendment

- Right to freedom of religion, speech, and press.
- Right to assemble peaceably, and to petition the government for a redress of grievances.

Second Amendment

- Right to keep and bear arms in common defense.

Third Amendment

- Right not to have soldiers quartered in one's home in peacetime without the consent of the owner, nor in time of war except as prescribed by law.

Fourth Amendment

■ Right to be secure against "unreasonable searches and seizures."

Fifth Amendment

■ Right, in general, not to be held to answer criminal charges, except upon indictment by a grand jury.

■ Right not to be put twice in jeopardy for the same offense.

■ Right not to be compelled to be a witness against oneself in a criminal case.

■ Right not to be deprived of life, liberty, or property without due process of law.

■ Right to just compensation for private property taken for public use.

Sixth Amendment

■ In criminal prosecution, right to a speedy and public trial by an impartial jury, to be informed of the charges, to be confronted with witnesses, to have a compulsory process for calling witnesses in defense of the accused, and to have legal counsel.

Seventh Amendment

■ Right to a jury trial in suits at common law involving over $20.

Eighth Amendment

■ Right not to have excessive bail required, nor excessive fines imposed, nor cruel and unusual punishments inflicted.

Ninth Amendment

■ Enumeration of certain rights in the Constitution shall not be construed to deny or disparage others retained by the people.

Tenth Amendment

■ The powers not delegated to the United States by the Constitution, nor prohibited by it to the states, are reserved to the states, respectively, or to the people.

*Source: *Our American Government*, U.S. Government Printing Office, Washington, D.C.: 1993.

Throughout the history of the United States, the Supreme Court has diligently protected the concept of individual freedom and continues to do so to this day. The protections afforded by the Constitution from the backbone of what liberty and freedom mean to the people of the U.S., and what attracts people to this country in great numbers.

These freedoms are not the freedom to do anything you please. You cannot infringe upon the rights of others, or put others in danger, but you can live knowing that there are protections in place that keep the government from treating you unjustly.

Many of the changes to the Constitution have been to extend freedom and protection to groups that were not included in the initial experiment of democracy. Over time, all of the legal rights of the Constitution have been given to women and minority groups, giving equal status to all the people of the United States, regardless of race, gender, or religious belief. This legal equality has been hard earned, often by protest or violence. In practice, there are still many lingering inequalities in how women and minorities are treated, but our culture is moving in a corrective direction (see the following chapters).

INDIVIDUAL PERSONS

The individual has always been idolized in our culture. Strong individual efforts have been captured in our early folk tales and glorified in our interpretations of history, and in our literature. Men like Lewis and Clark, Daniel Boone, and Davy Crockett, who helped the westward settlement of the country, are characterized in American folklore as rugged adventurers. The accomplishments of famous cowboys like William "Buffalo Bill" Cody, Wyatt Earp, "Doc" Holiday, Judge Roy Bean, William "Bat" Masterson, Wild Bill Hickok, and Pat Garrett have been captured in romantic western tales. There were also women who captured the spirit of the "Wild West"; for example, Calamity Jane and Annie Oakley were contemporaries of William Cody. Harriet Tubman was a conductor for the Underground Railroad.

Native Americans, who have often been cast negatively, had their icons as well. Geronimo, Sitting Bull, Crazy Horse, and Black Elk were leaders who witnessed the devastation of their own cultures as a result of the westward expansion of the United States. The history of Native Americans is long and rich and has had its darkest days in the last three hundred years. Today their voices are contributing productively to the current dialog of race and ethnicity in our culture.

American public opinion is traditionally very sensitive to such issues as the image of "underdog," which is often attached to people and groups struggling for their independence. People in the U.S. have had an almost equal fascination with the outlaw. Famous outlaws like Butch Cassidy and the Sundance Kid, Clay Allison, Black Bart, William "Billy the Kid" Bonney, the Dalton Brothers, John Wesley Harden, and

Jesse James were all either thieves or murderers that have been roman-ticized in print and film. This continues today as we embrace individuals who push the edge of our society. Movie, sports, and music celebrities are now fulfilling those roles, and several of our Presidents' popularity increased almost in direct relation to their infidelities and their indiscretions.

The influence of the "larger than life" hero and anti-hero runs throughout our history and is reflected in the culture that we experi-ence today. The values reflected by the powerful, reckless, adventurous, and potentially deadly lone individual have continuously been reborn or reinvented in our culture. From the early adventures—cowboys and American Indians—to the gangsters of the 1930s and 40s—to the rebel-lious youth of the 1950s—to the civil rights protesters of the 1960s—to the anti-war demonstrators of the 1970s—to the politicians, entertain-ers, movie stars, and entrepreneurs of the 1980s and 90s, all in some way can be identified as individual heroes, heroines, and outlaws.

PEOPLE IN SOCIETY

Americans are not always viewed positively around the world. In some cases, when traveling abroad, they deserve and reaffirm negative stereo-types due to their behavior, although there are times they don't deserve the labels. They particularly may not deserve the stereotypes that are the result of what one sees in the media. We—as people in a large society—are not reflections of the media any more than the media is a reflection of us.

The United States is seen around the world as being the land of oppor-tunity. It is viewed as a place where someone can begin with relatively lit-tle, and through hard work, ingenuity, and dedication rise to riches. This has

> ## For class discussion
>
> What is your view of people from the United States? Do you have stereotypes or generalizations about how these peo-ple are? What drives those impressions? Make a list of the (a) positive and (b) negative characteristics of the people of the U.S. and discuss the source of these impressions.

been true for a few people, but for most it is a life of "ups and downs," just like everywhere else, and sometimes people do not win the big jack-pot in the end (or even a small one).

For the most part, the United States is a country that is made up of hard working people. There are rich and poor individuals; howev-er, the dominant population is made up of middle class working folk just like the authors of this book (and we are proud of it!). It is the breadth and depth of the middle class that makes this country so productive. However, for a nation that is so rich and so giving to the rest of the world, it has a great deal of poverty, as well.

Many international students are surprised when they come to the U.S. and see that some people are living in poverty or on the streets. This is a reality of our culture and we are working on ways to serve the poor and get them into a position that they can help themselves.

For class discussion

What is the "American Dream" and what does "Keeping up with the Joneses" mean? When you find definitions and explanations, try to illustrate them with some examples.

For those that can't make it, people offer help through religious and community groups. Government social programs are also in place to serve as a net and offer a helping hand.

The United States is a capitalistic country and it does consume a great deal of resources compared to the rest of the world. In addition, it is a country made up of communities that actively celebrate life and have traditional festivities. The country has many organizations that operate through volunteer help and these operations generally do a lot of good for people.

The family is still the primary unit of the culture and it is highly valued, even though every family may not look or behave in the same ways. There are people in the U.S. who are religious, as well as those who are not, and they all get along for the most part. Those that are religious can usually find a variety of churches, mosques, temples, and synagogues from which to choose. For those that aren't religious, there is separation of church and state that frees people from having religion imposed upon them.

INSTITUTIONS

The U.S. society is made up of individuals, families, communities, and other institutions that create the fabric of its culture. Education, religion, local, state, and federal governments are examples of such institutions. The media, the military, and corporate enterprises are other examples. Institutions have a powerful influence in this country. From the outside it may look as if the U.S. is all about its institutions and how it can make them bigger, better, and more complex. Many international students have commented on how institutionalized everything seems to be in the U.S. This might seem to be inconsistent with our underlying emphasis on the individual, but our institutions actually serve as a frame for American individual icons.

We have always had many institutional heroes. For example, the presidential families of Franklin and Eleanor Roosevelt and John and Jacqueline Kennedy served as cultural icons in politics and this extended into other aspects of society. The military leaders Ulysses S. Grant, Dwight David Eisenhower, and Colin Powell are a few of the many institutional leaders whose accomplishments carried them into political leadership. Billy Graham, Pat Robertson, Pat Buchannan, and Jerry Falwell have been dominant voices in organized religion. Dr. Martin Luther King was the spokesman for the civil rights movement of the 1960s, and Jesse Jackson has continued to carry the civil rights torch that was ignited by Dr. King. Albert Sloan, J. Paul Getty, Donald Trump, and Bill Gates are representative of business as an institution, and Orson Wells, Barbara Walters, Oprah Winfrey, and Walter Cronkite have been spokespersons for the media. These people, and many others too numerous to mention, serve as role models with whom other people can align themselves when they speak for their representative institutions.

As mentioned earlier, the U.S.A. is undeniably a capitalistic country. The institutional structure of the United States is complex and very well integrated with the market economy. More and more we are seeing corporate alignment with existing institutions. In education, the influence comes in many forms: from advertising in public schools, colleges, and universities to driving research in some universities. In addition, many institutions often have to make the choice between Coke and Pepsi, or between IBM-type PCs, which are driven by Microsoft's operating system, and Macintosh, which is an Apple Corporation product. The implications of the choices that large institutions make in these proprietary type decisions can mean large profits for corporations like Coke, Pepsi, Microsoft, and Apple.

In professional sports, it is very clear whose support any given team receives. Watch any event and you will see the high profile of corporations. Many professional sports and arts facilities are named after their corporate sponsors. For example, in 1999 the Washington Redskins football team reached an agreement on a 27-year, $200 million-plus

---

A homework assignment

Your assignment is to watch fifteen-minute segments of at least three different kinds of sporting events. Take notes on the number of corporate advertisements and the ways in which they were presented. Bring your notes to class for discussion. Generally, the weekend is a good time to see sports programming (baseball from March through October, football from September to January, basketball from November to June, ice hockey from October to June).

deal with Federal Express—the overnight package delivery service—for the naming rights to the team's Landover stadium. This means that until 2027 the stadium will be renamed FedEx Field. These types of contributions by corporations might be seen as intrusions; however, no one else is standing in line—particularly the government—to offset the billions of dollars contributed by corporate sponsors.

ART, MUSIC, LITERATURE, SPORTS, AND OTHER MAJOR ACHIEVEMENTS

The culture of a country is very often captured in its art, music, literature, scientific achievements, and, to some extent, by the other ways in which it entertains itself. Today, the people who are successful in providing entertainment in our society have been socially elevated by those of us who are entertained. Movie people, sports figures, musicians, television personalities, comedians, and super models are treated in many ways as a sort of royalty. Madonna, Mel Gibson, Oprah Winfrey, Deon Sanders, Michael Jordan, Chris Rock, Jewel, Bobby Brown, Back Street Boys, Mariah Carey, Cher, Tom Cruise, Nichole Kidman, and Julia Roberts are ushered in and out wherever they go as if they were heads of state. Their talent has afforded them wealth and privilege in our culture, and our children, for better or for worse, see them as role models. Chapter 9 covers the media and will develop this idea further.

The United States offers a rich variety of arts and many styles that are recognized today internationally have roots in the U.S. Music forms like jazz, the blues, soul, rhythm and blues (R & B), disco, country, and rap are firmly rooted in our culture. The United States has much to offer in the arts, some of which pushes the edge, some of which is conventional, and most of which shows a mastery of genre.

The chart below categorizes several artistic areas and some of the representative artists. Do you recognize any of these names? Try entering some of these names into the search engine of your Web browser to find samples of their work.

CAMPUS CULTURE

Many of the artists in the chart were in some way part of or supported by institutions of higher education. In many communities, the college or university is the primary provider of cultural activities. Become aware of the activities on your campus and make the effort to experience those activities. Studying is very important, but it is the

Artistic Area	Selected Contributors
Writers, Nineteenth Century	Mark Twain (Samuel Clemens), Ralph Waldo Emerson, Henry David Thoreau, Herman Melville, Nathaniel Hawthorne, Edgar Allen Poe, Washington Irving, Ambrose Bierce, and Henry James.
Writers, first half of the Twentieth Century	John Steinbeck, F. Scott Fitzgerald, Ernest Hemingway, Willa Cather, James Baldwin, John Dos Pasos, William Falkner, Kay Boyle, Eudora Welty, Ralph Ellison, James Thurber, Sherwood Anderson, Katherine Anne Porter, Sinclair Lewis, and Harriet Beecher Stowe.
Writers, second half of the Twentieth Century	Flannery O'Connor, Eldridge Cleaver, Joyce Carol Oates, John Cheever, Bernard Malamud, Kurt Vonnegut, Toni Morrison, Saul Bellow, Donald Barthelme, John Barth, William Styron, John Updike, John Irving, Amy Tan, T. Coraghessan Boyle, Alice Walker, John Casey, Ann Beattie, Tom Robbins, John Grisham, Erica Jong, Tom Clancy, Stephen King, and Anne Rice.
Playwrights	Arthur Miller, Richard Greenberg, William Inge, David Mamet, Tennessee Williams, Eugene O'Neill, Thornton Wilder, Lillian Hellman, George Kaufman, Neil Simon, Wendy Wasserstein, Beth Henley, Christopher Durang, Andrew Lloyd Webber.
Poets	Walt Whitman, Elizabeth Bishop, James Wright, Richard Wilber, Adrienne Rich, Anne Sexton, Sylvia Plath, Margie Piercy, James Merril, Phillip Leviene, Robert Hayden, Allen Ginsberg, Emily Dickinson, Lawrence Ferlinghetti, James Dickey, Gwendolyn Brooks, Robert Bly, Elizabeth Bishop, C. K. Williams, Maya Angelou, and Langston Hughes.
Painters	James McNeill Whistler, Gilbert Stuart, John Stewart Singleton Copley, Norman Rockwell, Andy Warhol, Mary Cassatt, and Georgia O'Keefe.
Photographers	Ansel Adams, Anne Leibovitz, Margaret Bourke-White, Berenice Abbott, Dorothea Lange.
Sculptors	Alexander Calder, Daniel Chester French, Helen Farnsworth Mears, Louise Nevelson, Malvina Hoffman, Anna Hyatt Huntington, Gertrude Vanderbilt Whitney, Isamu Noguchi.
Architects	Frank Lloyd Wright, Louis Sullivan, and Henry Richardson.
Dancers and Performers	Fred Astaire, Ginger Rodgers, Gene Kelly, Josephine Baker, Isadora Duncan, Katherine Dunham, Suzanne Farrell, Martha Graham, Pearl Primus, Gregory Hines, Helen Tamiris, Michael Jackson, Paula Abdul, and Janet Jackson.
Composers	John Phillip Sousa, Aaron Copland, Francis Thorne, Meredith Monk, George Crumb, Elsa Maxwell, Kay Thompson, Carrie Jacobs Bond, Amy Beach, Laurie Anderson, Mary Lou Williams, and Frank Zappa.

"other" things that colleges and universities provide that many people reflect upon as being the most influential on them as a person.

Most institutions will charge you an "activities fee." This is generally a required fee that is used to enrich the cultural and social activity of the campus. Also, many institutions provide social and orientation events for new students, and some provide social events specifically for international students. You may initially feel very alone when you arrive in the United States; however, you must be aware that there are three groups on most campuses in which you will automatically belong.

The first will be the group that is formed by the other incoming international students. You will more than likely come in with a cohort of young men and women from all over the world. You all will be experiencing similar issues and despite the diversity of the group, you should immediately identify with some of its members. The second group consists of the existing international students who are at various stages of cultural adjustment. These students can be very helpful for your orientation and for mentoring you as a new international student. Don't be afraid to ask them questions. Their answers may be the most valuable ones you can get, as they have been through the same experiences through which you will be going.

Finally, the third group of people you will identify with will be the students from the United States who have lived or studied in other countries themselves. They have been through the process of adjusting to another culture and also readjusting to their own culture. Many of these students are very comfortable with international students and some may have lived in your country. Often these students belong to campus groups called "Global Nomads." Information about Global Nomads can be found at their website:

http://globalnomads.association.com

Colleges and universities are at minimum communities, and some of the larger universities are like small towns. They have their own character and culture. There is a lot going on and a wide spectrum of activities from which to choose.

Many institutions, for example, take great pride in their athletic programs. It is up to you to take advantage of this and go to sporting events to cheer your team on. There is nothing like the energy of a stadium or coliseum full of cheering people. Catch a play at the campus theater or a concert by the campus orchestra. If you feel that you are talented in a particular area, take that talent to the appropriate department and let it be developed. International students have made great contributions in the intellectual and cultural life of college campuses in the United States. Don't miss out!

Chapter 7

Gender Roles

W hen the sociology professor asked the students to express their opinion about the reasons for a high divorce rate in and among American families, Sony quickly raised his hand. When he was called, he said that—in his view—most of the problems in the American family take place because women have too much power. "Freedom of action and individualism are poor substitutes for responsibility, respect, and sense of duty," he added. He also said that in America so many women are preoccupied with their own personal issues, such as equality, that they forget about their responsibilities as mothers and daughters.

Sony did not expect that his words would cause such criticism from several students in the class. They angrily replied that for many years equality and freedom have been the most important issues for which American women have been struggling. One student called Sony's opinion "sexist," another suggested that he think before expressing such views in class. Sony left the classroom confused. After all, he did almost exactly what the professor had asked—he had simply tried to express his opinion. He went to the professor's office to ask for his advice. What bothered Sony was that he believed his liberty to speak was a sacred right in America.

"No, do not be afraid," commented the professor. "Nobody should limit your right to speak. However, you have to understand that there are some views that most Americans consider inappropriate and some of them would vigorously defend what is considered right to them. We touched a very delicate issue: gender roles. Very often how you express your ideas is as important as what you say. Try to learn more about issues related to equality between men and women, sex bias, and sex discrimination. These views can be quite different from those that are accepted in your home country, and that is okay. I will not say that you should embrace what most Americans consider to be right. I simply want you to learn more about gender roles. In fact, your goal is to learn, correct?"

In this chapter we will explain essential facts concerning gender-related behavior and gender roles in the United States. We will share with you basic information about the societal relationships between men and women, major social policies related to women, and especially those guiding principles that promote equality between the sexes.

SOME DEMOGRAPHICS

As in most countries in the world, in all categories of the U.S. adult population, there are more women than men (see Table 7.1). Some social scientists suggest that women are expected to live longer than men because of genetic and other biological factors.

TABLE 7.1   Overall number of women and men in the United States, estimated. (*Source:* Population Estimates Program, Population Division, U.S. Census Bureau, Washington, D.C., March 1999.)

GENDER	NUMBER	MEDIAN AGE
Women	139,785,000	36.7
Men	133,616,000	34.4

However, most experts refer to other, non-biological reasons that affect higher death rates among men. For example, men traditionally occupy more dangerous and risk-related jobs, such as in public safety and the armed forces. Also, there are more fatal car accidents involving men than women, and men are more likely to be engaged in aggressive, reckless, and risk-taking behavior (Schubert, 1991). In addition, psychologists explain that women are better able to cope with stress and frustration than men are and this may also explain why the life expectancy for women is higher (see Table 7.2).

TABLE 7.2   Number of U.S. men and women over 65 and 85 years of age, estimated. (*Source:* Population Estimates Program, Population Division, U.S. Census Bureau, Washington, D.C., March 1999.)

GENDER	65 AND OVER	85 AND OVER
Women	20,287,000	2,961,000
Men	14,364,000	1,256,000

According to the U.S. Bureau of Census, approximately 25 percent of adult Americans (over 18 years old) are not married. About one-third of married couples live without children (the couple either does not have children or they have children elsewhere who have already left the family). Approximately one-quarter of American adults live with their children. In the 1990s, approximately 2.4 million marriages took place in the United States every year. However, there were also about 1.2 million divorces (dissolution of marriages) per year.

On average, American women in the 1990s had two children. This statistic varies, however, among various groups. For example, African-American women have approximately 2.5 children, and Hispanic women (South and Central American origin) have approximately 3 children per person. The overall tendency is that the higher the income and educational level of a woman, the fewer children she has.

For many years in the United States, men provided a greater percentage of the income to the family than women. This tendency began to change after the 1950s. However, there is still a significant gap between men and women in terms of their earnings (see Table 7.3).

Median annual income of men and women in the U.S., age group over 15. **TABLE 7.3**
(*Source:* Money Income in the United States. U.S. Census Bureau, Washington, D.C., 1998.)

GENDER	NUMBER	MEDIAN ANNUAL INCOME
Women	96,694,000	$14,430
Men	94,948,000	$26,492

There can be several explanations why the earnings gap between men and women exists. For example, more women than men have part-time jobs or occupy temporary and low-paying positions. This is primarily because they have small children and cannot or do not want to be employed full-time. Also, as you see from Table 7.4, more men than women have earned doctoral degrees. Typically, a higher academic degree produces more income. The lower degree you have, the lower salary you are likely to get. There is also evidence that men receive more financial compensation for the same job than women do. In addition, there are unwritten practices that may favor men over women in terms of promotions. This hidden discrimination against women has caused the U.S. government to begin taking steps to guarantee women equal protection under the law. In most employment cases today, the relationship between the employer and employee are regulated by special rules supported by federal and state laws. We will get back to them shortly.

TABLE 7.4 Educational attainment of persons 15 years old and over.
(*Source:* U.S. Census Bureau, Washington, D.C., 1998.)

GENDER	BACHELOR'S DEGREE	MASTER'S DEGREE	DOCTORAL DEGREE
Women	15,231,000	4,639,000	515,000
Men	14,859,000	4,656,000	1,355,000

SEX, GENDER, AND EQUALITY

Before we begin our dialog on gender and equality, we should briefly explain the differences between the words *sex* and *gender* in the way that they are understood today in the United States. **Sex** refers to the biological and anatomical differences between males and females. A newborn baby can be identified by the child's sex as being either male or female. **Gender** refers to socially constructed differences between men and women based on societal norms and values. Newborn males and females acquire their roles and become boys and girls, and then men and women.

Probably the most important social and political issue in the relationship between men and women in the United States is equality between sexes. There is formal equality, in terms of legal rights, and there is practical equality. In many countries, the law guarantees equal opportunity and many other types of equality for men and women. However, practically, men have more power, more rights, better access to resources, and, therefore, better opportunities than women have. Let's explore some examples.

There are almost universal divisions of labor between the sexes. Overall in the world, significantly more men than women work in public and professional spheres. There are significantly fewer men in such areas as child education, child rearing, and homemaking. In many cultures, a newborn girl is considered as less "valuable" than a newborn boy. Social roles, stereotypes, and expectations continue to influence the process of development of both men and women.

American Public Views on Equality

Americans had to go a long way before their attitudes on equality between the sexes began to change. Egalitarian attitudes—those views that support equality between men and women—did not "suddenly" occur in opinion polls. In 1936, for example, only 36 percent of Americans believed that there should be more women in politics. Less than a third of Americans in the 1930s favored a possible appointment of a woman to the Cabinet. Even in the late 1960s, only half of Americans supported the idea of a woman candidate for the presidency (Erskine, 1971).

The situation has changed dramatically since the beginning of the 1970s. A 1984 Gallup Poll found that nearly nine out of ten Americans would vote for a woman candidate for mayor, governor, or Congress (Gallup, 1985). This trend has continued through the 1990s.

A class exercise

What is your view on gender roles? Are you egalitarian or traditional in your views? Please indicate your opinion regarding the following statements by circling the answer closest to your feelings. The numbers in brackets indicate the number of points you get for each answer.

1. If a couple lives together, who should do most of the housework, like cleaning, cooking, decorating, and washing?
   Mostly she [2]   Both equally [1]   Mostly he [0]

2. If a couple lives together, who should have more freedom of action: she or he?
   Mostly he [2]   Both equally [1]   Mostly she [0]

3. If a couple can afford two cars, a new model and a 1989 model, and both work just 5 miles from home, who should drive the newer car?
   Mostly he [2]   Both equally [1]   Mostly she [0]

4. If a couple's child gets sick with a cold, and one of the working parents—who are equally busy—should pick up their sick child from school, who should do it?
   She [2]   Hard to tell [1]   He [0]

5. The family budget should be generally under the control of:
   Husband [2]   Both spouses equally [1]   Wife [0]

Add your scores. If your score is between **8 and 10,** your attitudes are traditional; between **0 and 2,** your attitudes are feminist; between **3 and 7,** your attitudes are egalitarian. See the website for details.

MEN, WOMEN, AND ATTITUDES

How different are men and women in terms of their views on particular social issues? Historically, women in the United States have been and are more opposed than men to the use of force. Women were also more supportive of gun control and opposition to capital punishment. Women showed greater support for school prayer, social help to the needy, jail terms for drunk drivers, bans on smoking, cigarette advertisement, and higher taxes on cigarettes. Women have been and are more likely than men to oppose legalized gambling, drug use, and prostitution. In addition, girls also have tended to hold on to the more idealized image of political authorities longer than boys. During the last thirty years, women have been more likely than men to support the Democratic presidents: Jimmy Carter in 1976, and Bill Clinton twice in 1992 and 1996 (Andersen, 1997).

Studies show that women tend to be more oriented than men toward local political issues, especially those pertaining to schools and education. Men, in contrast, show greater interest in national and international affairs. Women's interests primarily include policies regarding equality, environmental protection, disarmament, education, culture, and social and welfare issues. Men's interests, however, included economic and industrial policies, energy issues, transportation, national security, and foreign affairs. In many countries around the world, first ladies traditionally accept roles of sponsors of the "arts and humanities" (Skjele, 1991). Young females are significantly more pro-equality than males, especially with regard to ethnic and racial prejudice (Sidanius & Pratto, 1993).

GENDER STEREOTYPES

Sex chromosomes or sex hormones are, of course, responsible for sex-related motivation. However, these biological factors are neither necessary nor sufficient to cause differences in behavior. Biological differences simply change the probability of occurrence of certain behavior. A remarkable survey was conducted in 27 countries (Williams & Best, 1982) in which people were asked to indicate whether particular words (adjectives) were closely associated with men, women, or not associated by gender. A general sex stereotype was present in all cultures. Cross-culturally, such characteristics as dominance, autonomy, aggression, exhibition, and achievement were associated with men. Such traits as nurturance (providing loving care and attention), help in time of distress, reverence, and abasement were associated with women. Males are seen as more robust, assertive, aggressive, autocratic, forceful, stern, and wise. Women are seen as dreamy, sensitive, affectionate, sentimental, and submissive in the overwhelming majority of rural developing countries (Williams & Best, 1990). In these societies, unlike in industrial nations, the perceived differences between men and women are greater than the perceived differences in industrial countries.

CULTURE AND SEXUALITY

Human sexual behavior is certainly regulated, at least in part, by human physiology. Hormones and other chemicals in our body influence sexual motivation. However, genes, hormones, and other biological factors just change the probability of occurrence of certain types of sexual behavior. Societal factors including laws, customs, and norms in fact determine what types of sexual behavior are acceptable, under what circumstances, and with what frequency. Every culture has its own set of requirements, beliefs, symbols, and norms regarding sexuality and its expression.

This set of characteristics is called **sex culture.** Sex cultures vary greatly across the world and are influenced by religious, ideological, political, and moral values developed by society. Therefore, the sex culture in the United States may be different from sex cultures in other countries.

What we consider sexual is determined by a combination of biological, psychological, and cultural factors. Many cultures consider sexual pleasure as normal, desirable, and natural, while others view it as primitive, sinful, and even abnormal. For instance, in many cultures there is a popular belief that masturbation is a sin that could cause retardation and other serious psychological problems (Kon, 1979). Although this view is not completely unknown in the United States, it is no longer popular.

Is it possible to accurately compare information about sexual behavior in America to other countries? We believe that such comparative information would mostly be inaccurate. Let us explain why. Cultural beliefs about sex, and individual beliefs caused by them, may affect the quality of research about sex. For example, the so-called refusal rate (proportion of people who do not want to participate in a study as subjects) may affect the validity of surveys on sexuality. Why does this happen? Because of the existing cultural norms of permissiveness, people in one country may be open to talk about sex, agree to give interviews, and answer survey questions. People who grew up in more sexually restrictive environments are often very reluctant to give away any kind of information about sex and their intimate life. Moreover, any conversations about this topic—even reading these pages—can cause embarrassment for some students!

For these and some other reasons, it is difficult to compare such criteria as premarital and teenage sex, extramarital sex, frequency and number of sexual relationships, or sexual abuse. For example, if we compare the numbers of reported sexual abuse cases in the United States to some other countries, these data are likely to be incompatible or biased. Why? Women in the United States—because of cultural and political traditions—are more likely than women in other countries (especially in developing ones) to report abuse against them. In many traditional countries, a woman may not report sexual abuse because it is considered dishonorable for the woman even to mention insults against them. The shame of self-disclosure and the fear of hurting their families in such cases is so overwhelming that women prefer not to tell anybody about their traumatic experiences.

Social values that regulate sexual motivation can be quite different across cultures. For example, chastity—no experience with sexual intercourse—is not regarded as a particular value among many young women in the United States and such countries as Sweden, Denmark, Germany, or Holland (the list can be expanded, of course). On the other hand, in such countries as Iran, India, Kuwait, and in many others, chastity is essential and vital for the woman's position in the society (Halonen & Santrock, 1995).

Traditional and Nontraditional Cultures

Sex cultures can be divided into two large categories, traditional and nontraditional. Traditional sex cultures endorse restrictive rules regarding the expression of sexuality among their members. These cultures also tend to suppress most forms of expression of sexuality. In contrast, nontraditional sex cultures are generally permissive, and tolerate different forms of sexual behavior. In such nations as the United States, Holland, Sweden, Russia, Australia, Denmark, and some other countries, sex does not carry the same mystery, shame, and conflict it does in more traditional cultures (see Table 7.5). Even a country's style of clothing may represent a particular sex culture. In traditional Islamic societies, women are typically veiled and cloaked from head to foot. On the other hand, contemporary European and American fashion trends allow women to expose most parts of their bodies. Those who visit European countries know that on most public beaches women may appear topless.

Type of sex culture and general attitudes toward specific issues. **TABLE 7.5**

ISSUES	TRADITIONAL SEX CULTURE	NONTRADITIONAL SEX CULTURE
Expression of sexuality	Heavily regulated	Somewhat regulated
Premarital sex	Prohibited and rejected	Somewhat tolerated
Extramarital sex	Prohibited and rejected	Somewhat tolerated
Homosexuality	Prohibited and rejected	Somewhat tolerated
Chastity	High value	Relatively low value

Labels of "traditional" and "nontraditional" can be misleading, however. Many people who live in traditional sex cultures could express attitudes and behavior that are more common in nontraditional sex cultures, and vice versa. Family socialization, attitudes, adulthood experiences, and many other environmental factors affect an individual's sexuality—including his or her thoughts about sex, frequency of sexual acts, and type of sexual activities. Attitudes may also change over a period of time. For example, almost 70 percent of Chinese respondents (China is regarded by many as having a traditional sex culture) did not denounce extramarital affairs. This is a higher percentage than the rate found in the United States. In fact, in the 1990s, about 50 percent of the Chinese respondents were believed to be engaged in premarital sex (Rathus, et al., 1993). On the other hand, in the nontraditional sex culture of the United States, many prominent figures—including popular senators, actors, and opinion leaders—raise their voice in support of traditional family values, chastity, and marital commitment (Edsall, 1998).

Different cultures may promote specific attitudes toward particular types of sexual lifestyles. For instance, homosexuality is tolerated in Western industrial societies. In studies conducted in the 1970s and 1980s, about 20 percent of American males reported at least one homosexual experience in their lives (Reinish, 1990). In approximately one half of the non-European societies, homosexuality was rare (Broude & Greene, 1976). It is virtually absent in the other half of non-Western societies. However, such statistics are difficult to verify because people in these countries, as we suggested earlier, may be either ashamed or afraid to tell about their sex life and orientation.

There are two basic understandings of the causes of homosexuality. According to one body of beliefs, individuals express homosexual behavior because it is motivated genetically; culture has only some impact on homosexuality. According to another opinion, referred to as the environmental approach, social and cultural factors are in large part responsible for homosexuality.

Cultural and political views on homosexuality vary. In the 1930s, homosexuality was a serious crime in Nazi Germany. Before the 1990s, it was a crime in the Soviet Union. Homosexuals in those countries were considered criminals and mentally ill, and were severely punished. For many years, even in the United States, homosexuality was considered a mental disorder. Only recently, in the early 1970s, based on the predominant opinion of American mental health specialists, homosexuality was removed from medical diagnostic manuals (DSM-IV, 1994). It must be understood that in the U.S., particularly on college campuses, there is a great deal of tolerance and acceptance for alternative views and choices in the area of sexual orientation.

SEXISM

What is sexism? This is behavior—an action or expressed opinion—that discriminates against women or men based only upon their sex or gender characteristics. It is important to make distinctions between sexist behavior and sexist opinions. Sexist behavior is, in fact, discrimination against women or men. Sexist statements, on the contrary, are not necessarily direct discrimination, but are often expressions of deeply embedded stereotypes. However, sexism is almost always divisive, no matter how it is displayed, be it in someone's actions or words. Let us give several examples of sexist actions.

- A professor at a state university announces that he will teach a new class in the fall semester. During registration he suggests to several female students who wanted to sign up for his class that they should take another class because this class will be more beneficial to men.

- The chairperson of a student organization on campus—a club that includes both male and female students—says that she has to have a deputy. Several male students express their desire to work for this organization; however, the chairperson says that the deputy has to be a female student because in her opinion, men are not as responsible as women are.

- A personnel officer of a security firm wants to hire someone for a building security-guard position. One man and one woman apply for the position. Both are equally qualified and have the same level of security-guard experience. The manager decides to pick the man because, in his opinion, men make better security guards.

- A manager of a small company needs to hire a secretary. Three people apply for this position: two men and one woman. They all have some experience and are qualified to work in the position. The manager decides to hire the woman because he believes women do secretarial work better than men.

- A single mother is refused a promotion in the company for which she works. As she explains it, the manager was afraid that because she had a child—and children do get sick—she would be unable to constantly be at work, an *assumed* requirement of the job.

- A newly wed young woman's job application is refused on the basis of her marital status. It is explained to her that she could become pregnant very soon and her absence from work—due to pregnancy and the birth of a child—would be unacceptable by the management.

- A teacher gives different homework assignments to the students in class. Male students receive difficult assignments and female students receive easier ones. The teacher says that he is doing this because women usually are not particularly "good" at this subject.

Sexism stands for the denial of equal opportunity for men and women. Nevertheless, do not think that any action that is made in favor of one gender over the other is sexist. For example, behavior in the cases below should perhaps not be called sexist. A careful observer with a critical mind can detect and understand contextual elements of human behavior. Let us examine some of them.

- A sports club is looking for a person to work as a janitor in the female locker rooms. There is no way for a man to get this position. Why is this case not discrimination against men? Because privacy rules require that there should be a woman working in the locker rooms designated for women only.

- No professional football team has signed any female players. This is not discrimination against women. Why? Because anyone who knows about professional football could argue that with only a few exceptions, most professional football players are recruited for the National Football League from college teams across the nation. Women do not play for any college-level football team, nor are there any well-known competitive female college football teams in the United States. All in all, playing college football is a prerequisite to playing professional football. (The sexism in this case probably could be identified in children's football leagues, middle and high school athletics, and possibly attributed to collegiate level football.)

- A movie director is looking for actors—men and women—for his new movie. A woman cannot be hired to play men's roles and a man cannot get the job to play a woman (in some comedies, however, such "substitution" may be appropriate).

In many cases and situations it is very difficult to establish whether a sexist act has been committed. People can offer differing interpretations of situations, and their views are based on their background, beliefs, and many contextual details. Let us give several examples of such controversial situations. What would be your opinion if you are asked to comment on these cases?

- A men's college soccer team needs a goalkeeper for the forthcoming season. Rama, a 19-year-old sophomore, says that she could play for the college team. She feels she has enough soccer experience playing goalie for her high school. The college, unfortunately, because of financial considerations, does not have a female soccer program or team. The coach refuses to accept Rama and the team continues to look for a male goaltender to fill the position.

Is this a case of sexism? On one hand, many of us would suggest that it is absolutely logical to expect that only men should play for men's sports teams. Yet Rama argues that the college's sports programs are supported by taxpayers' money, and it is fundamentally unfair to deny her membership in the team just because she is a woman. Therefore, her logic may be compelling for many individuals. For example, in Little League baseball, which is designed by local communities specifically for younger children, there are only teams for boys. However, recently it was established in court that girls should not be denied the opportunity to join these baseball teams. Today if you look carefully on the fields where seven- to ten-year-old children are playing baseball, you are likely to see a girl or two playing on the team.

- Anyone who buys a car in the United States must purchase automobile insurance. If a man and a woman own identical cars and their driving records are similar, the man will pay higher monthly premiums than the woman.

Is this discrimination against one sex? Some may readily say yes, because men are required to pay more because of their sex, right? Not completely. According to statistics, men are involved in more destructive automobile accidents than women and this is costly for the insurance companies. Therefore, men are charged more money by the insurance companies not because they are men, but because they are more dangerous drivers than women!

A class exercise

Please express your opinion about whether the cases discussed below portray sex discrimination. Your opinions will be based on your personal experience, beliefs, and values—there are neither correct nor incorrect answers here.

CASE 1.   The restaurant owner is looking for a female waitress to work evening shifts. This restaurant attracts many single men; therefore, according to the owner's opinion, another female waitress would be good in terms of both sales and tips. The owner has hired men to wait tables before, but the results were not great.

CASE 2.   The publisher of a women's magazine is looking for candidates to fill the position of senior editor. Among several qualified applicants there is one man, whose candidacy is rejected outright because the publisher says that a man cannot be an inspirational leader for a female periodical. The magazine publishes materials related to some sensitive women's issues in the United States and the world.

CASE 3.   Due to a number of circumstances, the department of biology in one private college is composed of six women and no men. All six female professors agree that it would be excellent if the department could hire a man for a new job opening. The selection committee decides to interview only male applicants.

CASE 4.   A television station in one of the big cities on the East Coast has a tradition of broadcasting the evening news with two news anchors working together in the studio: a man and a woman. When the female anchor is promoted, the station starts looking for a woman with professional experience to fill the position. Any man who applies for the opening will have much less chance to get the job because the station is looking specifically for a woman. Nevertheless, do you think that this situation is an example of discrimination? Explain your position.

Sexist Remarks

Perhaps you have heard, "This is a sexist statement," or "This person has made a sexist remark." In the opening vignette for this chapter, Sony's views were called "sexist." What is a sexist remark? How do you recognize these kinds of remarks and avoid using them? A sexist statement is an expressed opinion that discriminates between men and women only on the basis of their sex or gender. Quite often the sexist opinion is not based on facts, or the facts are limited or not verifiable. Sexist statements are very general, simplistic, and may seriously distort the truth about men and women. It is also important to have in mind that sexist statements typically degrade one sex in favor of the other. Therefore, most sexist statements can be offensive and may cause a change in the way the listener views the person making the sexist remark. Following are several examples of sexist statements and an explanation of their meaning.

- "Women cannot work under pressure, while men can."   This is a sexist statement because we all know that both sexes can work well under pressure. Moreover, research suggests that very often women are able to cope with stress better than do men.

- "Women are better parents than are men."   This is a sexist statement because there are good fathers and good mothers and who determines which one is better? Moreover, the person who made this statement did not identify what "better" is.

- "Men are irresponsible."   As you can see, this is an unsupported generalization. What is responsibility and what is the context of this comment? Is there evidence that most men are irresponsible? The statement is too vague, and therefore can be considered sexist.

Now consider the following sentence. "Women live longer than men." The statement is obviously bad news for most men. However, emotions should be put aside. Why? Because this is absolutely true. The life expectancy for a woman, around the world, is higher than a man's life expectancy, and the difference can be as much as 10 years in some countries! Some facts are difficult to accept. Sorry, men!

AFFIRMATIVE ACTION

American law prohibits any discrimination of individuals because of their race, color, religion, gender or national origin. Born of the civil rights movement in the 1960s, affirmative action calls for women and minorities to be given special consideration in employment, education, and business decisions. Judging by the results today, the playing field appears to continue to be tilted very much in favor of white men. Overall, minorities and women are in vastly lower-paying jobs, and still face active discrimination in some sectors. The proponents (supporters) of affirmative action say that equal opportunity cannot be just an empty slogan or an expression of good intentions. Equal opportunity should be achieved by legal and political means (Hill, 1997). This policy is implemented to increase diversity in business, education, and social activities. In its modern form, affirmative action can call for an admissions officer, faced with two similarly qualified applicants, to choose the minority over the white, or for a manager to recruit and hire a qualified woman for a job instead of a man. Defenders of affirmative action say that granting modest advantages to minorities and women is more than fair, given hundreds of years of discrimination that benefited mostly white men.

However, these days an increasingly assertive opposition movement argues that favoring members of one group (women, for example) over another (men, for instance) simply moves discrimination from one group and imposes it on the other. This situation is often called "reverse discrimination." Critics blame affirmative action for robbing them of promotions and other opportunities. They argue that free competition and the marketplace itself would promote those individuals who can contribute to community and society, without giving these people special treatment.

The United States Supreme Court has limited affirmative action and suggested that affirmative action can be used only where there is ongoing discrimination against minorities and women. Some states, California, for example, are moving to abolish affirmative action in education and job recruitment. Behind the defiant rhetoric lies a political and legal quagmire—the changing view in U.S. courts and public opinion of affirmative action, in general, and set-aside programs, in particular. Since 1989 the U.S. Supreme Court has held that city governments may use set-asides only as a last resort; otherwise, the court has said such preferences may not be based on race or gender.

SEXUAL HARASSMENT

We have mentioned that freedom of speech is one of the most fundamental freedoms that Americans have. However, there are situations in which particular words are not considered proper, and may be rejected and condemned by many people. This is not the government's attempt to restrict free exchange of ideas. On the contrary, certain limitations aim to protect people—and you would be one of them—from the harmful words and actions of other individuals. For example, in your communication with other people in the area of human sexuality and male-female relationship, there are general rules you must follow, a violation of which might be considered sexual harassment. Traditionally, exchange students ask many questions about this issue. Therefore, in this chapter, we will clarify several important things that one should know about this issue and your rights as a student and human being.

What is sexual harassment? According to the U.S. Equal Employment Opportunity Commission, **sexual harassment** is a form of sex discrimination that violates Title VII of the Civil Rights Act. It typically includes unwelcome sexual advances, requests for sexual favors, and other verbal or physical conduct of a sexual nature. This conduct affects another individual's employment, interferes with his work performance, or creates an intimidating, hostile, or offensive work environment. The college or university that you attend will have an institutional policy related to sexual harassment, and it should be highlighted in the student handbook. This is a serious topic on campus today, and there is little tolerance for sexual harassment. Sexual harassment can occur in a variety of circumstances. Let us discuss some of them.

- *Student "R" tells a sexual joke (the content of the joke includes male and female genitalia and sexual intercourse) to a group of students, both male and female; most of them do not know Student "R" well.*

  This joke could be offensive to some or maybe all students in the group—and it does not matter how many male or female students there are in the group. This situation definitely fits into the category of sexual harassment.

- *Student "U" whistles loudly as he walks across campus and sees a beautiful woman passing by.*

  Even though such behavior may not be uncommon in many countries, and even in some movies, this qualifies as sexual harassment.

- *Student "P" talks to a female student he met two days ago, telling her how beautiful and sexy her body is.*

  If two people are not in a relationship, any mention about a woman's body (that includes breasts, hips, legs, lips, and other parts of the body that may represent female sexuality) is inappropriate. This is particularly inappropriate if such comments are made in a public place. By the way, the same rule applies to women's comments about men's body parts. Remember, the victim (a person who is harassed) as well as the harasser may be a woman or a man. Boys may be sexually harassed by girls. The June 1993 Harris Poll found that 57 percent of boys who have been harassed have been targeted by a girl, 35 percent by a group of girls. The kinds of examples boys give include comments on the size of their private parts, jokes about the extent of their sexual experience, being called "gay," and unwanted grabbing of their buttocks (Stein & Sjostrom, 1999). The victim also does not have to be of the opposite sex. In other words, a male can harass another male.

- *Student "A" and student "Y" met in class a month ago. They are not friends. "A" asks "Y" to help her with the homework assignment. Student "Y" agrees but jokingly suggests that "A" should return the favor in the way that women always return favors to men.*

Such innuendo about sex, especially as a form of "payment" for help—even though it is said in the form of a joke—is offensive to another person and causes significant distress. In this case, "Y" uses his knowledge in the academic subject as a form of interpersonal power.

- *Student "T" tells a student at a party that "T" is the sexiest man alive because he belongs to a particular ethnic or national group.*

Again, even though the statement may be considered a tease, it may be seen by some as a direct solicitation of sex. Moreover, because it was said to a particular student directly, it may be interpreted as an act of sexual harassment.

- *Student "W" makes a public remark about Student "J" in which "W" says with laughter that "J" might be gay.*

The sexual orientation of another person is his or her private issue and cannot be discussed openly, without this individual's explicit consent. Sexual teasing, ridiculing, and mocking are forms of sexual harassment.

- *Student "L" talks to another student (they met only last week) and touches her neck and ear when they are in line for dinner.*

This is improper behavior. Even though "L" believes that the relationship is going well, he still has to first ask about what is acceptable and what is not in his behavior.

Useful tips

Try not to tell sexual jokes or make remarks about other people's sexual activities and body parts associated with sexuality. If you do not know the person very well, but want to communicate with him or her, ask this individual what remarks, gestures, or opinions are offensive to this person. Do not assume that rules of communications between men and women that are acceptable in your home country are equally acceptable in the United States. If there is something that you cannot comprehend well, talk to your instructors or to those who have lived in the United States for a long time.

Please remember, sexual harassment is not always intentional. It can be unintentional, spontaneous, and designed to be comical. If you say, "I did not want to offend this individual," it doesn't mean that you are not responsible for your words. In addition, sexual harassment is always interpreted from the victim's standpoint. You may say that your remarks were not inappropriate, but what is judged is the effect of the words! Sexual harassment is not always a direct discrimination or intimidation. It can be subtle, hidden, and covered by words with double meanings.

You may say, "How can I remember all these rules of behavior?" You do not have to remember. What you have to do is understand the ideals behind the rules and agree with them. Then your memory will help you to recall the details. Meanwhile, some useful tips that might help you learn more about sexual harassment are summarized in the box.

It is helpful for a harassment victim to directly inform the harasser that the conduct is unwelcome and must stop. The victim of sexual harassment should not be afraid to complain about a harasser. If you think that you are right, do not be afraid that the person you accuse would deny your words. There may be other people who have similar complaints against this individual.

A homework assignment

Determine which of the following statements are sexist and which represent true facts. If you don't know the answer right away, search for facts on the Internet or ask your instructor for assistance. The website contains some possible interpretations.

1. "Women in the United States are more vulnerable to eating disorders than men."
2. "There are more single mothers in the United States than single fathers."
3. "There are more violent criminals among men than among women."
4. "Women do not drive as well as men."

Chapter 8

Ethnicity, Race, Religion, and Adjustment

People often do not realize how much discomfort and frustration simple words can cause. In 1999, when Britain's Prince Philip, husband of Queen Elizabeth, was visiting a high-tech company near Edinburgh, Scotland, he spotted a poorly wired fuse box. He immediately threw a remark to the company manager: "It looks as though it was put in by an Indian." Perhaps the Prince wanted to say something funny and did not want to offend anyone. Unfortunately, he did offend. You can imagine how offensive this "joke" was to millions of hard-working Indians living around the world. It is true, people can laugh at many jokes and often do not mind being called funny names. However, one of the most sensitive topics for many of us is our origin. Misunderstandings, verbal, and written mistakes can destroy friendships, cause distress, and even retribution from other people. How can one prevent such negative developments? We believe that one of the solutions is your knowledge about other people and their origins. In this chapter we will take a closer look at nationality, ethnicity, religion, and race in the United States.

By the way, the royal spokesperson later apologized for Prince Philip's clumsy remark.

RACE AND ETHNICITY: BORN OR BRED?

We often hear these words: race, nationality, and ethnicity. What meaning do people in the United States attach to these words? To begin with, we should say that there is no "official" or "correct" understanding of these terms. Our usage of these and many other words and expressions is based on how most people interpret them at a certain point in history. Therefore—and also because American sociologists and anthropologists are still debating about the definitions of race and ethnicity—we will introduce the most widespread, common, and prevalent views on these terms. It must be understood from the beginning of this study that race and ethnicity is a significant, powerful, and emotionally charged issue in the United States, and that much social commentary and controversy surrounds this issue.

Race is usually defined by most specialists as a group of people distinguished by certain similar and genetically transmitted physical characteristics. It is essential to comment on the high or low frequency of occurrence of such physical (related to body) characteristics because practically all physical traits appear in all populations. For example, some Germans have frizzy hair and some Africans have red hair. There are many dark-skinned European Americans and light-skinned African Americans. Many American experts, however, suggest that race is better described and understood as a social category. Why? Primarily because race indicates particular experience shared by many people who belong to a category of people that is called *race* (Gould, 1994, 1997; Langaney, 1988). Some people have proposed to abandon this word altogether, while others offer to use the word "origin" (for example, African or European) instead of race.

Today in the United States, the government, as well as many private organizations and agencies, often ask anybody who applies for a job in their organizations to identify their race or origin. Several standard categories are identified:

Whites or Caucasian (includes people of European, Arab, and Central Asian origin)

Blacks or African American (includes people of African origin)

Native American (includes people of American Indian, Eskimo, and Aleut origin)

Asian (includes people of East Asian and Pacific Islander origin)

Hispanic (includes those whose origin is Chicano, Mexican, Mexican-American, Cuban, Spaniard, Puerto Rican, or the Spanish-speaking countries of South or Central America or the Caribbean)

RACE/ORIGIN	POPULATION BY 2005

U.S. population by 2005 (estimates). **TABLE 8.1**

(Data: The U.S. Bureau of the Census, Current Population Reports, Series P25-1130, *Population Projections of the United States by Age, Sex, Race, and Hispanic Origin: 1995 to 2005.)*

RACE/ORIGIN	POPULATION BY 2005
All Races	285,981,000
White (including Hispanic)	232,463,000
Hispanic origin (of any race)	36,057,000
Black	37,734,000
American Indian, Eskimo, and Aleut	2,572,000
Asian and Pacific Islander	13,212,000

For detailed information about continent and country of birth of the foreign-born population in the United States, see Appendix 3.

How many people of each race or origin live in the United States? Table 8.1 offers estimates made by the U.S. Bureau of Census—a government organization that provides statistical analysis of the American population—of the distribution of races in the United States by 2005.

Does the place of our birth or ancestral origin make us different in terms of behavior, emotions, or values? Most specialists in human behavior say no. What makes us relatively different—or relatively similar—is our experiences accumulated during childhood, adolescence, and adulthood. Let us illustrate this thought using the following examples.

Ramesh was born to his dark-skinned and dark-haired parents from India. His hair and skin are dark too. Ramesh's parents speak English with an Indian accent. He speaks the language without a detectable accent and enunciates words almost like a national news broadcaster. Although Ramesh's parents adhere to many traditional Indian values and beliefs, Ramesh in most ways reflects typical beliefs and customs of American teenagers. This description implies that humans are born with the basic dispositions created by an interplay of genetic factors. People then develop their individual attitudes, skills, and other attributes under the influence of their culture.

For example, a loaf of bread is not just a mixture of flour, salt, and water. It takes a baker's effort to bake it. On the other hand, the loaf is not a result of the baker's wish: one cannot bake bread without having its ingredients. The final product (bread) is the result of the baker's effort: he or she transforms the existing ingredients into the loaf of bread. Biological factors—for example, the way your nervous system functions—constitute the *foundation* for our behavior. Social and cultural factors, childhood experiences, the overall situation in society, family practices, education, traditions, and many other influences determine who we are as adults.

One of the most significant factors that affects human lives everywhere and creates disparities of many kinds among people is availability of resources and money. Higher income, for example, guarantees better opportunity for a person. If Mary has better opportunities in life than Susan does—a better house, higher quality food, better access to education—then Mary has a greater potential to have a higher-paid job. Better opportunity can produce higher income. Higher income creates more opportunities for those who earn this income compared to those who do not. Look at Table 8.2 and compare median household incomes of American families.

TABLE 8.2 Median income per household, 1998.
(Source: U.S. Census Bureau, Current Population Survey, March 1998. Median scores in this table indicate that 50 percent of the families in each category make more than the median score and 50 percent of the families make less than the median score.)

All races	$38,885
White	$40,912
Non-Hispanic White	$42,439
Black	$25,351
Asian and Pacific Islander	$46,637
Hispanic origin	$28,330

Which group in the United States has the highest income per family? Which group has the lowest? In general, who would have better economic opportunities in the United States?

Because various social groups share common experience—such as wealth or poverty, norms, symbols, religion, values, and memories—the individuals of a particular group are expected to have some typical psychological traits, somewhat different from the members of another culture or group. However, human groups are extremely diverse and there are tremendous behavioral variations within them. For instance, in the primarily materialistic and individualistic American culture, there are many philanthropic and idealistic people. Likewise, in primarily collectivist cultures, one can find selfish, greedy, and arrogant individuals.

In the United States, the term **ethnicity** usually describes your cultural heritage, the experience shared by you and other people who have a common ancestral origin, language, traditions, and, often, religion and geographic territory. A **nation** is defined as a people who share common geographical origin, history, language, and are unified as a political entity—an independent state recognized by other countries: for example, those who acquire the status of a national of the United States—who become citizens—are either born in the United States or become citizens through a naturalization process.

There is a lot of confusion in the way people across countries use the words race, ethnicity, and nationality. What is often labeled as "race" or "ethnicity" in the United States is termed "nationality" in some other countries. For example, if Ron, who refers to himself as being an "African American," marries Lilia, who refers to herself as a Latina (a popular description of one's Hispanic origin), their marriage

A useful tip

Ethnicity and Nationality in the United States

It is important to realize that the United States, like most nations, is made up of many different ethnic groups. Similarly, there can be different national groups within an ethnic group.

Same nationality, different ethnic groups.

Martha and Martin are both U.S. citizens. Nationally, they are both Americans. However, ethnically, Martha is Brazilian, because her parents emigrated to the U.S.A. from Brazil when she was a little girl and she received her citizenship a few years ago. Martin is a seventh-generation New Yorker. His ethnic roots are mixed: Irish, French, German, and Russian.

Same ethnic groups, different nationality.

Hamed and Aziza are both Palestinian exchange students living in New Jersey. Hamed's parents live in Tel-Aviv and both he and his parents are Israeli citizens. Aziza does not have a permanent nationality, even though she holds a Jordanian passport.

would be labeled an interracial marriage in the United States. The same marriage would be labeled either cross-national or international in some other countries. Moreover, one can easily find racial categories common in the United States that are not recognized in Panama, Brazil, or South Africa—to name a few—where they might have a different understanding of what race is.

We should not forget that human groups are constantly moving and mixing with others. In the United States, perhaps more frequently than in other countries, people have freedom to chose what cultural identity they want or have and what group they want themselves to be identified with. Phenomena such as ethnic or national identity are becoming increasingly dynamic and are based on different interests, ideas, and choices of the individual.

Language influences our attitudes about other people and affects our evaluation of different ethnic groups. Americans, as you know, enjoy one of the most fundamental civil liberties—freedom of speech. In particular, it is against the law for the government—with some exceptions, like threats to other people's lives—to punish American citizens, residents, and guests for what they say, write, or wear. However, there are many cultural norms and standards that suggest the type of words considered to be appropriate, and what words are perceived as offensive and, therefore, inappropriate. Most colleges and universities have special regulations that limit the use of offensive language in the classroom—called ethnic or racial slurs—particularly if the person is using the words in an attempt to offend other individuals. One must be *very* careful when referring to racial groups in a public dialog, as it is very easy to offend someone by a naïve or outdated use of a term.

Are there language standards related to the names of various ethnic groups? Cultural standards and unofficial norms in the United States change over time. For example, consider the ways in which names applied to various ethnic groups have changed and continue changing. Some terms look appropriate and others appear less appropriate in television reports, newspaper publications, books, and

A useful tip

Learn how people label ethnic groups and groups of origin (race). Enjoy freedom of speech; however, be sensitive to what other people feel about certain words and expressions about them. You may hurt others without intending to. Ask questions, like "Is it okay to use this word?" Some people do not like to be labeled by ethnic categories, but prefer to be referred to by the country of their origin, for example, "Brazilian," "Korean," or "Nigerian," but not "Latino," "Asian," or "African."

everyday conversations. What values might be implied, for example, in the use of "Indian" or "Red Skin" versus "Native American"? There is nothing particularly special about these three terms. However, the terms "Indian" and "Red Skin" are derogatory and demeaning labels. The term "Native American" sounds more familiar and is far more appropriate for the year 2000. We commonly say "Oriental food," but most prefer to say "Asian," referring to a person from China, Vietnam, or Korea. The word "Hispanic" is an official term used by the U.S. government to refer to people of South or Central American origin. However, many Hispanics prefer to be addressed as "Latino" (men) or "Latina" (women). A long time ago, in the 1880s persons of African descent were referred to as "colored" or "Negro." These labels were commonly used. However, in the 1960s, many critics suggested that these labels were debasing and inappropriate (Berry & Blassingame, 1982). The terms "Black," "African American," and "persons of color" became most commonly used by the end of the twentieth century.

RELIGIOUS BELIEFS

Religion gives many of us meaning and purpose in life. It teaches us about the most appropriate rules of conduct and provides us with powerful self-restraint against inappropriate behavior. Religious beliefs help us cope with many tragic situations in life and give us an emotional boost during personal defeat, failure, or downfall. Religious beliefs are inspirational, and they help us overcome obstacles and keep our hopes alive.

Almost 90 percent of Americans identify with a specific religion. (General Social Surveys: 1972–1996). The United States is home to many of the world's religions. As you may know, Pilgrims, the first European settlers in America, came to this country with a particular religious vision. Moreover, back in Europe many of them were subject to discrimination, persecution, and—quite often—physical extermination. Today, as throughout American history, individuals who are persecuted in their home countries for their religious beliefs and practices can receive asylum in the United States.

Which religions have the most followers in this country today? Please look at Table 8.3 below.

As a free individual you have the right to choose any religion, or no religion. The U.S. Constitution permits private religious activity in colleges and universities. However, certain rules and regulations apply to any religious activity in the United States. These rules are general-

TABLE 8.3   Major U.S. religions, 1999.

(Source: Yearbook of American and Canadian Churches, 1999; D. Kendall, 1999, *Sociology in our Times.* ITP: New York.)*

RELIGIOUS BODY	NUMBER OF MEMBERS
Protestant (Christian)	85,500,000
Roman Catholic Church (Christian)	61,207,914
Muslim	6,000,000
Orthodox Christian (Russian, Greek, Ethiopian, and others)	5,631,000
Jewish	5,602,000
Church of Jesus Christ of Latter-day Saints (Mormons)	4,923,100
Buddhist	1,864,000
Hindu	795,000

ly the same for both public and private schools. However, some private institutions of higher education may have their own guidelines about religious behavior on their campuses (check, for example, www.ed.gov/Speeches/04-1995/prayer.html).

All in all, in the United States, government and religion are separate. Therefore, state-funded colleges and universities will not have courses in their curricula designed to promote any particular religion. However, you may find courses on the history of religion, comparative religion, and others that teach about the role of religion in the history of the United States and other countries.

You have the right to pray individually or in groups. You are free to discuss any religious views with your peers, so long as these discussions do not cause disruption of public order. There is nothing wrong with discussing honesty, hard work, compassion, respect for the rights and freedoms of others, respect for property, civility, friendship, and peace. You enjoy the right to read any religious scripture, say grace before meals, pray before tests, and discuss religion. However, your school activities come first. For example, you should not pray during the test for an hour and then ask your professor for extra time to finish the test.

Can you express your religious beliefs in the form of projects and reports? Yes, you can, and no one should reject your work because of its religious content, such as quotes, symbols, and examples. However, your work should be relevant to the assignment given to you. Follow the instructions and guidelines. These guidelines usually mention the grading criteria for your work, such as substance, relevance, appearance, and grammar. For example, if your sociology professor gives an assignment to find and compare suicide rates in several countries, you may not claim an exemption from the assignment because suicide is strongly prohibited by your religion.

If, during a class discussion, you are asked about a particular military action, and if you oppose that action based solemnly on your religious beliefs, can you make religious remarks on the issue? Yes, you can. Your remarks during classroom discussion constitute your expression of free

> ## A useful tip
>
> Any criticism against a particular religion should not be excessive. In this case, such criticism may be called religious harassment.

speech. Similarly, you can criticize religion and promote atheistic views. Your professor may not silence you just because you make critical statements against religion. However, do not forget that other students also have the right to speak and they may criticize your views, too.

You also have the right to distribute religious literature to your schoolmates. Nevertheless, you are supposed to do this only in a particular place, at particular times. Use common sense and talk to professors and counselors if there are any problems or unanswered questions about religion on campus.

You are protected by law to observe and speak to others about the religious holidays you celebrate. You can talk about religious traditions, practices, and history of those religious holidays. Feel free to invite other students to join you in your celebration. However, if students decline your invitation, do not insist, because it may be considered harassment. As you see, harassment can be of two types: pro- and anti-religion.

In many cases, your school will excuse you for participation in religious celebrations and rituals, especially if it requires your absence from school. However, the school is not obligated to do so, and if you miss a test or an assignment you will be held accountable. Do not assume that your particular religious practices will be given priority over the published academic schedule. A brief list of common religious holidays is outlined in Table 8.4.

Religious messages on T-shirts, shirts, and hats are not generally prohibited on campus. Students may wear religious attire, such as crosses, yarmulkes, turbans, and head scarves. If your religious beliefs do not allow you to wear gym clothes because they are too revealing, you may not be forced to do so.

TABLE 8.4   Brief description of some common religious holidays.

(Sunset times are calculated for Kansas City, Kansas, using the Sunrise/Sunset/Twilight and Moonrise/Moonset/Phase website provided by the Time Service Dept., U.S. Naval Observatory, which is the official source of time used in the United States.)

CHANUKAH (JEWISH) DECEMBER 3–11

In 179 BCE, the Maccabees led a group of Jews in battle against invading warriors who had desecrated the Temple and extinguished its eternal light. After winning the battle, legend has it that they found a single cruse of oil, which miraculously lasted eight days, until more could be found. The Chanukah menorah is lit for eight nights to celebrate the miracle. Chanukah was declared a holiday by Judah Maccabee and his followers to celebrate the rededication of the Temple. Gifts are exchanged and foods fried in oil are customary.

CHRISTMAS (CHRISTIAN) DECEMBER 25

This is the celebration of the birth of Jesus Christ, the Son of God, according to Christian beliefs. Many Christians attend a midnight Mass or other Christmas Eve services at churches that are usually decorated with poinsettias, candles, and greenery. Before Christmas children write letters to Santa Claus, a "gift-giver," and tell him what they'd like to receive for Christmas. With help from his elves, Santa prepares the gifts and on Christmas Eve he leaves the North Pole in his sleigh to deliver the gifts. Usually, the children of the house leave cookies and milk for Santa.

EASTER (CHRISTIAN) THE EXACT DAY OF EASTER VARIES EACH YEAR
BUT ALWAYS FALLS BETWEEN MARCH 22 AND APRIL 25.

Easter celebrates the resurrection of Jesus Christ, the most joyous occasion in Christianity. According to Christian belief, after Jesus was crucified by Romans and buried, Jesus' tomb was found empty. An angel told his followers that Jesus had risen and ascended into heaven. Many churches hold sunrise services on Easter Sunday to symbolize the return of light to the world after Jesus' resurrection. The day is observed with feasts and celebrations. Easter also marks the end of Lent. One of the Easter customs is egg painting and decorating.

RAMADAN (MUSLIM) OCCURS IN THE NINTH MONTH OF THE
ISLAMIC LUNAR CALENDAR. NOVEMBER IN 2001 AND 2002.

Ramadan is the most sacred holiday of the Muslim year and the holy month of fasting. Fasting is considered to be a very important form of religious

(continued)

Brief description of some common religious holidays (continued). **TABLE 8.4**

obligation of Islam and provides many benefits, including learning self-control. During this period, Muslims must abstain from food, drink, and sexual intercourse from dawn until dusk each day. Ramadan is a time of worship, reading the Qur'an, charitable acts, atonement, and the purification of individual behavior. Ramadan ends with the Festival of Fast-Breaking, which is a joyous celebration marked by a special gift of charity. Muslims dress in holiday apparel and attend a community prayer in the morning.

YOM KIPPUR (JEWISH) CELEBRATION IN 2001:
SEPTEMBER 27; 2002: SEPTEMBER 16.

Yom Kippur is the holiest day in the Jewish calendar. The observance is also known as the Day of Atonement since the events of Yom Kippur focus on asking and granting forgiveness for one's wrongdoings. Yom Kippur falls at the end of the 10 Days of Penitence, a period that begins with Rosh Hashanah, the Day of Judgment. Jews attend services at a synagogue or temple on the eve and day of Yom Kippur. On Yom Kippur, Jews perform no work and abstain from food, drink, and sex.

MAWLID (MUSLIM) 12TH DAY OF THE MONTH OF
RABI AL-AWWAL IN THE MUSLIM LUNAR CALENDAR.

Mawlid al-Nabi is a celebration of the birthday of the Prophet Muhammad, founder of Islam. Muhammad was born about A. D. 570 and died in A. D. 632. The Mawlid al-Nabi was first observed around the thirteenth century and was preceded by a month of celebration. The actual day of Muhammad's birthday included a sermon, recitation of litanies, honoring of religious dignitaries, gift giving, and a feast.

DIWALI (HINDU) THE FIFTEENTH DAY OF KARTIKA.

Diwali is a five-day festival. The celebration means as much to Hindus as Christmas does to Christians. Diwali means "rows of lighted lamps," and the celebration is often referred to as the Festival of Lights. During this time, homes are thoroughly cleaned, lamps are lit, and windows are opened to welcome Laksmi, goddess of wealth. Gifts are exchanged and festive meals are prepared. Because there are many religions in India, there are also many manifestations of the Diwali festival.

For more information about Federal and state rules and regulations regarding religious activities on campus, contact your school's counseling center or department of education in your state.

STEREOTYPES AND THE POWER OF GENERALIZATIONS

We often do not have enough time or patience to analyze every event we encounter, or every person we are dealing with. We categorize, pigeonhole, and classify almost everybody we see or communicate with. Such clear-cut opinions about other people are called **stereotypes.** In particular, a stereotype is a categorical assumption that all members of a given group have similar distinctive traits. Some people say, "Mexicans like rhythm," or "Canadians play hockey," or "Americans care only about money." However, not all Mexicans love rhythm, there are plenty of Canadians who do not like hockey, and not every American considers money his only concern in life! Such stereotypical beliefs as "most illegal immigrants are criminals," or "interracial marriages are less stable than same-race marriages," or "all Jews are wealthy" may be expressed in our daily judgments despite the fact that they are basically wrong. Of course, there are some undocumented aliens who commit crimes, but they represent a small

Cultural sensitivity

Politicians sometimes make embarrassing mistakes and offend people who they do not want to offend. For instance, during a speech about the conflict in Northern Ireland, President Clinton put aside his prepared written speech and put together an improvisation: "I have spent an enormous amount of time trying to help the people in the land of my forebears in Northern Ireland get over 600 years of religious fights. And every time they make an agreement to do it, they are like a couple of drunks walking out of the bar for the last time—when they get to the swinging door, they turn right around and go back in again and say, 'I just can't quite get there.' It's hard to give up these things." Although the President said he meant only to explain how difficult it is for ethnic groups to settle the conflict, the metaphor was upsetting to some Irish communities because it reinforced stereotypes about the linkages between Irish people and alcoholism. Some people even suggested that it was an "offensive and insulting remark to the people of Northern Ireland" (Pearlstein, 1999). Clinton later apologized for these impromptu remarks.

proportion of all undocumented aliens in the United States. The interracial marriage is as stable as the same-race matrimony. There are both rich, middle income, and lower income Jewish people.

You may say that stereotypes are really descriptions of large groups of people; therefore, one should not be offended by stereotypical judgments: they are related to thousands of people! We often use stereotypes, however, and apply them to individuals on the basis of national, ethnic, religious, or some other group affiliation! In such situations, we not only commit mistakes of judgment, but may also offend someone, since no one likes to be stereotyped. Please look at the example on page 160.

Why Do Stereotypes Occur?

Stereotypes arise largely out of our lack of knowledge about the people with whom we interact. Many stereotypes are produced because we often move no further in our communications than the first impression. People's "looks" are the easiest to recognize at a first glance. Therefore, some national, ethnic, or racial characteristics appear to be more salient and notable than other characteristics, such as education, age, or social class (Gudunkust & Bond, 1997). If a person feels angry or frustrated, negative stereotypes about other people come to mind easily. Moreover, we often use stereotypes to justify particular negative feelings about other individuals (Zaller, 1992).

Is there any evidence that racial and ethnic groups share similar psychological or behavioral characteristics? Some experts believe there may be. According to one author (Phinney, 1996), African Americans share such characteristics as emotional energy, experiences of collective survival, special time perception, and interdependence in relationships, especially within the extended family. American Hispanics, according to Phinney, display interdependence, conformity, and sacrifice for the welfare of their family members. They try to avoid conflict in interpersonal situations and are likely to show strong attachment, respect, and loyalty. They also have more flexible attitudes toward time than Europeans do. Phinney also suggests that Asian Americans maintain harmony in relationships, put the group interests over individual interests, feel the importance of duty, especially obligations to the family. What do you think about such categorizations? They are, of course, interesting and entertaining. However, these depictions are nothing less than sophisticated stereotypes about large social groups. Stereotypes simplify reality and allow us to make mistakes in our judgments of individuals.

A topic to think about

The following is a description of interpersonal communications of "typical" American, Japanese, and Arab individuals adapted from a best-selling book (Julius Fast, 1970, *Body Language.* New York: Pocket Books).

There are distinct differences in the way American, Japanese, and Arab individuals handle their personal "territory." In Japan, crowding together is a sign of warm and pleasant intimacy. Like the Japanese, the Arabs tend to cling close to one another. Arabs' houses are generally large and empty, with people clustering together in one small area. Arabs do not like to be alone, so that partitions between rooms are usually avoided. The Arab likes to touch his companion, feel him. The Japanese avoid touching, however, and prefer to keep physical boundaries. Typical Americans set "boundaries" in public. They avoid pushing or intruding into the space of another person. Americans very seldom shove, push, and pinch other people in public. Arabs have no concept of privacy in a public place. When two Arabs talk to each other, they look each other in the eyes with great intensity. The same intensity is rarely exhibited in the American culture.

Question. Do you think all these statements are stereotypical? Or maybe you suggest that these judgments are somewhat accurate. How should we draw a line between being accurate and being stereotypical?

Is it possible to reduce the impact of stereotypical judgments about other people? We hope that it is. In order to do it successfully, let us understand better the stereotypical judgment itself.

We make at least two mistakes when we make stereotypical judgments. In the course of evaluating similarities and differences between two groups, we often:

■ allow genuine differences to be obscured by similarities

■ allow genuine similarities to be obscured by differences

Stereotyping is, in fact, permitting similarities between phenomena to eclipse their differences. Those who stereotype other individuals and groups are prone to automatically overestimate "in-group" similarities, while minimizing (or even ignoring) "in-group" differences. In other words, the individual perceives group members to be more alike than they really are (for example, people of this ethnic group are always late for class) and, at the same time, does not recognize many of the ways in which they are different from one another (there are plenty of students in this ethnic group who are never late).

Moreover, groups we like and groups we do not like are seen as more different than they really are. In its most extreme form, this process is a fundamental component underlying prejudice, bigotry, chauvinism, and racism wherein all members of the particular "out-group" are seen as essentially the same, while their individuality goes virtually unnoticed.

Let us consider, for example, interpersonal interaction. Imagine you meet a person from an ethnic group that is different than yours. You may perceive a man or woman from this group as basically the same as every other individual from that group. In this way, you view people as not being distinct and varied individuals, each possessing a separate and unique constellation of life experiences, memories, feelings, perceptions, values, beliefs, hopes, fears, and dreams. Instead, these traits are spontaneously filtered through your own sociocultural stereotypes, from which they emerge as Koreans, Blacks, Jews, Latino, Vietnamese, and so on. In this environment, then, irrespective of an individual's unique situation, problems, or needs, you would offer essentially the same "cookie-cutter" approach to your communication.

Stereotyping is making erroneous judgments. However, do not reject the possibility that people can share similar behavior, emotions, or attitudes. How many times have you heard someone make the fol-

Think critically

Looking for both similarities and differences can be constructively applied in the cross-cultural counseling setting. For instance, members of the same cultural group may be different in virtually every personality trait. And despite apparent drastic differences, two individuals may share things in common. Consider the following brief vignette as an example of a search for commonalities in two people.

Student: "There's no way that you can understand how I feel. After all, you are American, and I'm not. And you've never been discriminated against because of your nationality."

Counselor: "You are right. I can never know exactly what it feels like. We are truly different in that respect. But at the same time, I know what it's like to be discriminated against because of my religion. And I have had the experience of being persecuted out of ignorance and hatred. To that extent, we do share a common experience. We are indeed both similar and different."

lowing pronouncement (or any derivation thereof): "You cannot compare these two people (from two different ethnic groups, for instance) because they are totally and completely different from each other!" This is a vivid illustration of someone making the converse mistake of allowing similarities between people to be overshadowed by their differences. Thus, the individual who staunchly and adamantly maintains that, "One should *never* stereotype," is effectively blinding him- or herself to authentic commonalities that actually do exist within specific groups. However, by obstinately clinging to this position, such individuals practically ensure that they will remain oblivious to true similarities within (as well as between) groups of people.

Similarly, counselors who tenaciously cling to the belief that, "Every student should be viewed and treated as totally unique and without regard to his or her cultural background," runs the risk of allowing true—and potentially helpful—similarities between persons to be overlooked, neglected, or omitted. Unfortunately, the counselor's overemphasis on individual differences typically is realized at the expense of minimizing interpersonal commonalities. As a consequence, for instance, deeply powerful and universal life experiences that appear to be intrinsic to the human condition—such as the need for love, acceptance, empathy, esteem, or meaning—are prone to be minimized, disregarded, or even outright rejected.

A useful tip

What we might anticipate from an individual based on our expectations does not often match with who he or she really is. Please be prepared for such inconsistency!

Stereotypes in Our Explanations

Stereotypes also occur because we try to explain other people's behavior. Imagine a man walking down a street who suddenly is hit by lightening. Who is responsible for this act of nature? According to a common tendency of judgment, individuals who are harmed by forces that are out of their control may still be held responsible for what happens to them. This is a universal tendency of human beings: to hold people somewhat responsible for the bad things that happen to them.

Why does this judgment occur? Perhaps we have great difficulty accepting the unfairness of life, or we have a strong need to believe that good is rewarded and bad is punished. This belief leads us to conclude that people get what they deserve, and deserve what they get: "What goes around, comes around," says the American proverb. These types of judgments are called attributions. Some examples of harmful attributions are offered below (Levy, 1997):

- "People in poor countries must have been responsible themselves for what is happening to them economically."
- "Rape victims must have behaved seductively before they were attacked."
- "Battered spouses must have had it coming to them."
- "Ethnic minorities must have brought prejudice on themselves."
- "Victims of religious persecution must be guilty of something, or they wouldn't be persecuted."

Stereotypes can influence our judgments about what in life is right and what is wrong. We get used to the "usual," every day things, to the point that we consider them normal, or natural. On the other hand, we pay close attention to things that appear to be new and unusual to us and may resent accepting them. This is how some stereotypes influence our behavior—we do not approve of many things that appear to be unusual to us, especially when we find ourselves in a new cultural environment.

People may feel, see, and hear things differently and make decisions that might appear inappropriate to people in other groups or countries. For example, the death penalty is banned by the law and opposed by public opinion in West European countries. However, in some other countries people not only support, but regularly attend public executions. Opinion polls suggest that most people in the United States support the death penalty, although the death penalty is legal in some states and not in others.

Stereotypes develop when we connect what we think is natural with what seems right, or when we proclaim that "things are as they should be." Or we presume that whatever occurs in nature is good because nature is in itself good. Consider beautiful palm trees on the seacoast, smiling children, and beautiful flowers! Hot tea with honey and fresh ocean breezes—if it is from nature, then it is inherently good! There is only one small problem; most of us are less inclined to mention examples from nature that we do not

A useful tip

The frequency of an event does not inherently determine its moral value or worth. Try to think critically. What is common, typical, or normal is not necessarily good; what is uncommon, atypical, or abnormal is not necessarily bad. Conversely, what is common is not necessarily bad, and what is uncommon is not necessarily good.

happen to like (Levy, 1997). What about birth defects and earthquakes? Or drought and famine? Hurricanes and monsoons? Are these phenomena any less a part of nature? Are they somehow "unnatural"? What we are doing is using double-standard judgments: we often embrace the "good" parts and ignore, dismiss, or rationalize away the "bad" parts. From a standpoint of morality, nature is just nature. People tend to impart particular values upon it.

Stereotypes: Defending Your Own Ego

Human beings are supposed to be rational. But we are not always so rational. In fact, sometimes we are not rational at all. Specifically, when our stereotypical opinions are being challenged, we are prone to feel that we personally are being challenged. When our views are criticized we may feel attacked and threatened! Our first impulse, then, is to protect our thoughts, as if we were protecting ourselves. As such, we tend to hold on to our opinions. We do it sometimes even when there is evidence to the contrary. We usually respond to such challenges by discounting, denying, or simply ignoring any information that runs counter to our beliefs. Here is an example of how people protect their stereotypes even in the face of contradictory evidence:

> *A useful tip*
>
> When faced with a discrepancy between your opinion and the facts, resist the natural tendency to assume that you are right, and the facts must somehow be wrong. That is, ask yourself directly in what ways your opinion might be wrong.

Person A. I know that all Mexicans who immigrate to the United States live close to the U.S. border.

Person B. But the facts tell a different story. According to the Immigration and Naturalization Service, more Mexican immigrants live in Illinois, a state located hundreds of miles north of Mexico, than in Arizona.

Person A. Either your statistics are not accurate, or those people are not really Mexican.

Stereotypes and Perceptions of Reality

Stereotypes and expectations based on those expectations create particular perceptions of reality. For example, take suicides: Which country—the United States or Sri Lanka—has the higher annual suicide rate? The suicide rate in the United States is 15 cases per 100,000 people. The suicide rate in Sri Lanka is 47 per 100,000—more than three times that of the U.S. Still, many people who do not know these statistics would assume that suicide rates are substantially higher in the United States than in most other countries. Why does such misperception take place? Partly due to the American media when they report various stories involving suicide, especially among celebrities. It is also assumed by some that western industrial countries should have higher suicide rates than the rest of the world because of such factors as stress and lack of emotional support in interpersonal relationships. Although these assumptions seem logical, they are only assumptions. They cannot explain the relatively complicated picture of suicide and its causes across the world.

Let's look at another question. Among the American poor (the yearly income of an "officially" poor person, according to government standards, is about $4,000 per person), which group is the largest: Whites, Blacks, or Hispanics? Some people would readily suggest Blacks or Hispanics. However, nearly half of all poor individuals are White, approximately one quarter are Black, and just under one quarter are Hispanic. Why might people be inclined to overestimate the proportions of poor racial minorities? Perhaps because these groups do, in fact, display disproportionately higher rates of economic hardship. Specifically, almost 30 percent of Hispanics and Blacks are living below the poverty level, while less than 10 percent of white Americans are poor (U.S. Bureau of the Census, 1997).

Is it possible to eliminate stereotypes? Some researchers are skeptical about it (Devine, 1989). Other specialists—and there are many of them—are more optimistic. It is possible to reduce the influence of stereotypes on our daily judgments if one accepts the view that human diversity could be greater than their sameness. Do not underestimate the extent to which your prior beliefs and knowledge can affect your current experience. Generalizations, especially concerning personality characteristics of members of other ethnic or religious groups, cannot be objective, impartial, or neutral. Become aware of your own personal values and biases about particular countries, religions, and ethnic groups. Avoid presenting your value judgments as objective reflections of truth. Remember that most ethnicity-related phenomena—such as traits, attitudes and beliefs—stretch out along a continuum; thus, it is both artificial and inaccurate to group them into categories! Stereotypes are often based on lack of knowledge and human ignorance. Open your mind, read, watch, listen, learn, educate yourself, travel, communicate—and you will reduce the impact of stereotypes on your life.

A class assignment

Stereotypes on a Cruise (adapted from Shiraev and Levy, 2001)

People may hold similar stereotypes about other people's behavior and habits. This exercise demonstrates how alike our perceptions can be. Imagine that you are on a cruise where you meet the following people: (1) a man from Japan, (2) a woman from Brazil, (3) a man from France, (4) a woman from Jordan, (5) a man from Germany, (6) a woman from Italy. You spend a great week in their company. Back home, you realize that your initial stereotypes about these people were confirmed. Can you identify the following behaviors with the nationalities described above? Complete the statements below please. Four hundred students in Virginia and Washington, D.C. also gave their assessments of popular stereotypes (see the website). Compare your answers with the most frequently exhibited stereotypes. Discuss other popular stereotypes in class. Pay attention to exceptions from stereotypical judgments.

Question: Who was this person (Japanese, Italian, French, German, Jordanian, Brazilian)?

1. This person was never late for breakfast, lunch, or dinner:
2. This person talked too much:
3. This person had three video cameras with him/her:
4. This person was the best *lambada* dancer in the group:
5. This person was drinking beer continuously:
6. This person was trying to date several people in your group:
7. This person was the quietest in the group:
8. This person kept smiling continuously and kept saying "yes":
9. This person said he (she) had never played poker and wouldn't be playing:
10. This person was drinking wine continuously:
11. Military marches were this person's favorite music:
12. This person said that after marriage he/she would love to stay home with his/her kids:
13. This person knew a lot about cheese:

Chapter 9

Media

Newspapers, Radio, and Television

Tell us what you watch, listen to, and read, and we will tell you who you are. The average adult American spends almost 1500 hours a year watching television. Radio was estimated to consume 1100 hours, recorded music 235 hours, and newspapers about 175 hours. One study estimated that the average American would spend the equivalent of nine years in front of the television by the time he or she reaches the age of 65 (Woodwards, 1997). You will better understand American life when you take a close look at what the average American person reads, listens to, and watches daily. This chapter will examine the mass media—television, radio, and newspapers—communication that is technologically capable of reaching most people in the country, and that is readily affordable to most.

Some people call the American media "Beauty," others call them "the Beast." Some admire the wide variety of choices offered by the media. Others say that they are too intrusive and dangerous. No matter whose view you support in this debate, you can make the mass media useful in your education. If you navigate through the 24-hour stream of news, articles, comments, opinions, and debates, you can expand your knowledge, as well as further develop your language skills. One important thing is required from you, however. Rather than just sitting and consuming the information, be an active observer, reader, and listener, instead. Special courses offered in many universities teach students about the American mass media. You will learn more about the subject, its history, development, and current state when you take such a course. On these pages, we will examine press, radio, and television only as educational sources, and suggest how to use them wisely for your personal development.

MASS MEDIA AND BUSINESS

Most facets of the American mass media are privately owned. Of course, public (not private) television and radio do exist in America. However, they are supported by local nonprofit organizations or are governmentally funded, like PBS on television and National Public Radio. Consequently, public media is not powerful enough to compete with private broadcasting corporations that can make billions of dollars a year. How do they make all this money? Revenues that run newspaper, TV, and radio business, as well as profits come almost exclusively from advertising. Commercial time and space are sold in America like any other product. Private newspapers, television and radio networks, and local stations need to have their audiences—the more viewers, listeners, and readers, the better. Companies want to advertise their products to as many potential buyers as possible. If many people, for example, watch a show, the more money will be paid by advertisers to run their commercials on this show. Therefore some shows, programs, and newspapers are more expensive for advertisers than others. A local newspaper will charge only a few dollars for an advertisement, whereas big market papers such as *The New York Times*, *The Washington Post*, or *USA Today* will charge thousands of dollars.

Popularity Ratings

Newspapers can easily measure their popularity by counting how many copies are sold during a month or a year. The popularity of radio or television can also be measured. Let us take television, for example. Two companies in the United States estimate, using scientific methods, the number of people tuned to various television channels and programs. The company named Arbitron has an agreement with 2,400 families all across the country and sends them special logbooks, where the participating individuals record what they watch and when. The other company, named A. C. Nielsen, has an agreement with 1,700 volunteers to install special electronic devices in their television sets. These devices record when the television is turned on and what channel is viewed. In other words, these randomly selected people, representing all ages, professions, incomes, and ethnic and racial groups in the United States, give information that reflects other viewers' interests in various television programs. Broadcasting companies learn from these reports not only what is most popular but also which groups like what programming: what is liked by men, women, children, what works for evening and for morning audiences. Notice that beer is advertised primarily in the evening and during sporting events. Toys and games are usually advertised during afternoons and early evenings, and primarily during children's shows. Evenings are more popular among the viewers than afternoons. Weekends attract larger audiences than weekdays.

What are some of the most popular television programs in the United States? In the 1990s, during different periods, popular shows included *Bill Cosby Show* (comedy), *60 Minutes* (public affairs show), *NFL Monday Night Football*, *Melrose Place* (drama), *Beverly Hills 90210* (drama), *Seinfeld* (comedy), *ER* (drama), *Friends* (comedy), and many others. Perhaps the most expensive advertising is during the Super Bowl, the final football championship game of the season, which usually takes place on the last Sunday of January. One can correctly deduce that the Super Bowl is one of the most watched events on American television.

Governmental Regulations

It is commonly said that the American media are overtly preoccupied with sensationalism, sex, and violence. Many Americans agree with this assessment, but others say that this is okay because the business is regulated by the laws of supply and demand. If you want to see a particular program, you turn your TV on. If you dislike the program, you switch the channel or turn the TV off. (Moreover, some say that nobody forces people to buy television sets in the first place.) Media companies try to create and select only programming that will attract larger audiences, so that advertisers will pay more money for commercial time. If nobody wants to see a show, sponsors will not pay for advertisement time on this show, and if there is no money, there will be no television.

In theory, the government cannot say what should be broadcast on radio and television or what should be published in newspapers. Do not think, however, that if American broadcasters are driven to get as large an audience as possible, they can say and display whatever they want. Although freedom of speech is guaranteed by the American Constitution, mass media are subject to a variety of governmental rules and regulations. Broadcasting on radio and television is regulated by a government agency called the Federal Communications Commission. All media are subject to *libel* laws, which holds broadcasters responsible for false information that defames or harms others. In addition to federal regulations, all media are subject to local laws regarding *obscenity*. Therefore, nudity, extreme violence, and verbal profanity are banned from most programming. In cases of controversial events, public discussions, or political elections, television stations must provide equal time to all sides participating in the issue. Personal attacks aired on television require that the attacked person has an opportunity to respond. One cannot advertise cigarettes and tobacco products, or "strong" alcohol beverages, like cognac or vodka (except beer and wine). If a station or company violates such rules, it can be penalized financially or can be forced out of business. Since 1998, all television networks are required to attach special ratings to their programming indicating potentially disturbing aspects (such as violence, sex, and language), and informing parents whether or not the program is suitable for children of a particular age.

NEWSPAPERS

The first daily newspaper began publication in Philadelphia in 1783. They were expensive and could reach only a limited number of people. With the improvement of paper manufacturing and the invention of the steam-driven printing press, newspapers became cheaper and thus more affordable to average citizens. With the 1830s and publication of *The New York Sun*, which cost only one penny, the new era of the mass media in the United States began. Still, most early American newspapers were partisan, i.e., they were supported by different political parties and groups. Politicians used particular newspapers that were loyal to them to broadcast their political ideas. Only by the end of the 19th century did the independent press begin to develop. Most daily newspapers paid special attention to local news. Only the more expensive, weekly publications focused on national and international news. With the growth of competition, newspapers began to pay attention to sensationalizing their stories. It was discovered that stories about violence, crime, scandals, and sex could be sold very well. The term "yellow journalism," which first appeared in the 1880s, stands for low-quality sensationalist journalism.

The demands of free-market competition caused continuous changes in the newspaper industry. Today, afternoon newspapers are practically nonexistent and morning newspapers dominate the market. Business mergers have led to most cities being served by only one or two major newspapers. Some specialists suggest that contemporary American newspapers are very homogeneous and less politically influenced in their coverage of the news. Why has this happened? Newspaper owners want to sell their publications to large audiences and, thus, try not to be partisan on particular political and ideological issues.

American newspapers are, in many respects, huge corporations that are managed according to the laws and traditions of big business. Approximately 11,000 newspapers are published in the United States and about 63 million newspapers are sold daily (DeFleur and Dennis 1994: 92, 131). Such large city papers as the *New York Times*, the *Washington Post*, and the *Los Angeles Times* have millions of subscribers in their areas. Such national newspapers as *USA Today* and the *Wall Street Journal* have a daily circulation of more than 2 million! The most popular weekly issues of *Time, Newsweek*, and *U.S. News & World Report* each sell more than 10 million copies per week. The most popular magazines that discuss politics and public policy are *New Republic, National Review, Foreign Affairs, Atlantic Monthly*, the *New Yorker*, and the *New York Review of Books*.

A class assignment

You can examine different styles used by newspapers by comparing, for example, the *New York Times* and the *Wall Street Journal*. Take two copies published on the same day. First, compare their front pages. Will you find any difference in terms of headline topics? Compare how many photographs each of the two newspapers display. Do these newspapers pay attention to local news? Compare how international topics are covered. What do these papers say about weather, the arts, and sports? Looking at the paper contents, can you deduce who is the most "typical" reader of each newspaper?

RADIO

The first American radio stations were established in the 1920s and quickly became popular. With their appearance, the newspaper monopoly of mass communications began to disappear. Today in the United States there are more than 12,000 radio stations that reach about 80 percent of the population (Woodwards, 1997). Practically every American household has a radio and most cars also have one. Radio is available inexpensively, compared to television or newspapers. Focusing primarily on local news, weather, traffic reports, and music, radio has changed somewhat since the 1980s due to the rapid increase of talk shows. This format was popular fifty years ago; however, the rapid development of satellite technology has eliminated geographical barriers, and many talk shows have reached the national market. A person called "radio talk show host" (sometimes there are two or more such hosts) spends three or four hours in front of the studio microphone. Most of these shows encourage the listeners to call in with questions or comments. This format is the sixth most popular radio format, behind pop music, country music, religious music, and "oldies" (music of the 1950s and 1960s) programs. Since the end of the 1980s, political talk shows have also become increasingly popular. As specialists suggest, most of the American political talk shows are conservative, or express views close to the views of the Republican party (Fiorina & Peterson, 1998). Among nonpartisan political news programs is National Public Radio, a noncommercial network, that offers news, discussions, and political analyses of domestic and international news.

Radio Personalities

At the national level, among the most popular radio broadcasters today are names familiar to virtually every American. Due to the varied nature of each talk show, people hold differing, often opposing, opinions about these radio celebrities. Below is a brief description of four of the most popular talk show programs in the United States. You can listen to them every day in most states. Check local newspapers or the Internet to learn more about the radio station and hours of broadcast. We list these personalities only as examples of nationally known individuals. We do not necessarily endorse the content of their shows but recommend familiarity with them for your information.

Don Imus has been a celebrity of morning radio since the 1970s. Every morning he has over 2 million listeners, most of them high-income, highly educated men and women (advertisers like this category of potential buyers). Celebrities and national political personalities are frequent guests on the show. One of the keys to his success is that Don Imus often says whatever shocking thing that pops into his head. Once chosen as one of *Time* magazine's 25 most influential people in America, Imus talks about politics, social problems, and local events. The overall tone of his show is deeply sarcastic. His language is simple and he speaks slowly. One of the weaknesses of his show is that he often refers to past and current events familiar only to people who carefully follow American politics and have substantial knowledge in American history. It will be helpful to listen to the show with someone who can answer your questions regarding the topics discussed on the show.

Dr. Laura is a daily program hosted by Laura Schlessinger, a professional psychologist, who taught courses at the University of Southern California and at Pepperdine University, near Los Angeles. This show is a popular "pop psychology" radio event-psychotherapy session followed by 20 million listeners. The format of the show is simple: Dr. Laura takes phone calls from listeners who ask questions about their own personal problems, such as jealousy, mistrust, extramarital affairs, violence, and many others. Every day, up to 50 thousand people all across America try to call the show. Only a few of them succeed at getting through to ask their questions (*U. S. News & World Report*, 14 July, 1997). Dr. Laura's conversational style is confrontational. She herself admits that her popularity began to grow only after she started getting tough on the air. She can, for example, be very rude to a caller and say unpleasant things about him. In most cases, she insists that people themselves—not other people in their lives—are the cause of their problems. Polls show that this view is popular among Americans today: personal character and responsibility, not excuses, should be taken into account when trying to solve our problems. This show is very easy to follow and understand. You can take a look inside some people's personal problems and learn more about the daily life of ordinary people.

Howard Stern is a famous entertainer and radio personality whose radio show is especially popular among young listeners. At the same time, Stern's nationally syndicated radio show has made him one of the most despised men in America. He is constantly accused of bad taste, rude language, and lack of respect for people. Among the most common topics discussed on the show is sex, and especially lovemaking aspects of sex. Howard Stern invites guests to his show who range from the homeless and mentally sick to celebrities and high-ranked politicians. It is not surprising to listeners when female guests are asked to take off their clothes (and some of them do). Questions about the most intimate aspects of the guests' lives are persistently asked. "I must have a sexual thought about women every five minutes. I would be intellectually dishonest if I didn't reveal that to the audience," said Howard Stern in an interview. "But so many people are threatened by the truth. I'm a shock jock and they're shocked by the truth" (cf. Schaefer, 1997). Howard Stern always emphasizes that his show is what people need to listen to in the morning, and if he was disliked by people, nobody would have turned their radios on. If somebody doesn't like his show, he shouldn't listen. When you ask people around you to tell you what they think of Howard Stern, you will find differing opinions. College students and other young listeners are more supportive of his show than other age groups. Some will say that Howard Stern is the best entertainer, "king of all media," as he calls himself. Others will say that you shouldn't listen to his show. You are free to make your own decision, of course.

Rush Limbaugh's talk show became national in 1988, and it can now be heard in over 650 markets across the country and throughout the world. In the 1990s, the Rush Limbaugh show reached over 20 million listeners per week. The format of the three-hour show is as follows. Rush opens the program with a monologue about several of the most important, from his viewpoint, events of the day. Then he begins taking phone calls and answering questions from callers. Occasionally, he stops taking phone calls and delivers a monologue about a particularly interesting or important political problem.

The Rush Limbaugh show is a blend of sarcasm, humor, and serious criticism targeting mainly American liberals and the Democratic party. As the host openly explains to his listeners, all incoming calls are screened by the show's staff assistant, who selects only those calls that reflect Rush Limbaugh's conservative views. Once a week, on Friday, people with different political views are given air time for their questions and comments. Ask people around you and you will find that this show is very divisive: people will express entirely different opinions about this program and its host. Some will tell you that it is a great show, whereas others will be upset that you even mentioned his name. Like many American broadcasters, Rush Limbaugh also tries to promote his ideas through his own books. In the 1990s, for example, he published two bestsellers, *The Way Things Ought to Be* and *See, I Told You So*, which together have sold 9 million copies. These books are still available in most bookstores across the country.

TV NETWORKS, STATIONS, AND CABLE COMPANIES

Now let us take a look inside the television industry. Many students say that they are confused about the anatomy of American television. Indeed it is a very complex system, a conglomerate driven both by public demands and private interests. But despite its complexity, television can be explained in a simple way.

You may have heard these terms *network, cable,* and *television station* many times and wonder if they really have different meanings. Let us begin with television stations. Often called local stations, these companies send signals through airwaves directly to your television antenna. Although a part of private industry, television stations are subject to heavy governmental regulation. Due to technical problems related to transmission and interference of television signals, the number of stations which a city or town can have is limited. Thus, big cities like New York, Los Angeles, or Chicago can have no more than ten stations. Smaller cities are allowed fewer stations. Cable companies, unlike TV stations, do not send signals directly to individual homes. Cable systems broadcast signals first to a community antenna. Then the signal is sent by wire to individual homes. According to governmental regulations, cable companies have to carry local stations. In addition, they can offer a huge variety of channels from other cities. Satellite technology has created opportunities for cable companies to broadcast and receive programs from around the world. Cable television reaches almost 70 percent of American households. Overall, there are about 3,000 broadcast television stations (Woodwards, 1997).

Television networks are private organizations based on contracts among a large number of stations, which are called affiliates. Television networks offer their affiliates various programs ranging from soap operas and movies to talk shows and football games. Each station makes decisions about what kind of local or network programs to air. The biggest American networks, NBC (National Broadcasting Company), CBS (Columbia Broadcasting System), and ABC (American Broadcasting Company) were founded more than 55 years ago. For many decades, the "big three" dominated American television, competing with each other. Recently the competition increased with the emergence of the Fox television network and many cable companies.

So what are you watching when you turn your television on? If you do not have cable service, you will be watching what is offered by your local stations: a mix of local news combined with programming offered by networks. In most places today, you will have access to at least four stations. Cable service is relatively expensive and may cost you from $30 to $60 a month. In most university dormitories, students pay for cable themselves. If you decide to pay, your local cable company will plug your television into the company's antenna. In exchange, you will be able to receive from 50 to 100 or more channels, including all local stations.

Television and Language Proficiency

Television is a great educational source, so be prepared to learn from it. Many interesting shows and programs are aired when you are not at home; so ideally, you must have a VCR. If you do not have one, this is not a problem: it is always fine to ask somebody you know to tape a program for you and then lend you the recorded material. Buy a couple of videotapes for your recording requests. You can watch the taped program at the library or a TV lab on campus.

Many channels provide a wonderful feature, called closed-captioning, which is a written transcript of everything being said during the broadcast, and it appears on the bottom of the television screen. This feature was created specifically for individuals who have serious hearing problems. However, millions of viewers with normal hearing use closed-captioning to help them better understand the spoken language. Using this television feature, you are able to read and understand words that you either missed or misunderstood. Closed-captioning can eliminate the problem of following somebody who speaks very fast, or with a difficult accent. And finally, closed-captioning may help you to learn to spell better: the words you hear are spelled on the screen!

Think critically

Closed-captioning may not be so helpful if you overuse it. The constant presence of printed words on your television screen may create a kind of psychological dependency. Instead of listening to the spoken words and attempting to comprehend as much as possible, your eyes will be looking for "little helpers" on the screen. Therefore a balanced combination is necessary: closed-captioning could be "on" for some programs and "off" for others.

Keep a piece of paper or a notebook with a pen near your television set. Create for yourself a useful habit: whenever you are watching television and hear an interesting expression, a new word, or a name, try to write it down. (If you do not write it down immediately after you hear it, we guarantee that you will forget it in several minutes!) After the program is over, or at a later time, get a dictionary and translate the words you have written down. Go over the list several times and try to memorize the words and their translations. Students who follow this simple advice say that it allows them to add from three to five words daily to their active vocabulary! (Many words may later be forgotten, of course, because they are not used in conversations or written assignments; but still these words remain in our memory and may be recalled.)

OBSERVE DIFFERENT CONVERSATIONAL STYLES. Turn your television set on and do some channel "surfing": go through all the channels you can receive. Listen to what people say on television. For many foreigners unfamiliar with the English language, everyone speaks English in the same way, but that is not true. Americans speak with different accents. There are also different styles of language communication: official or formal, conversational, professional, and so on. If you want to be proficient in the language, you will have to learn more about the existing styles.

It will be difficult for you to compare different American accents while watching television because you do not have direct access to thousands of local stations across the country. Besides, even though there are noticeable accents, like New York, Texas, Louisiana, Boston, Minnesota, and others, television announcers and news anchors seldom speak with a strong local accent. What might be interesting is to observe different styles of conversation and communication. For example, observe the style used by television professionals who read the morning or evening news on the major networks: their speech is usually fast, smooth, nonrepetitive, and often filled with examples and colorful comparisons (check also *CNN Headline News*, as an illustration). If a show is designed for children (check, for instance, Nickelodeon in the early evening, or the Cartoon Network), notice how slowly everybody speaks on these programs. Do not be embarrassed to watch the children's shows: the language there is not filled with professional jargon and the spoken sentences are usually very short. By contrast, look at the nightly discussions on MSNBC, especially when lawyers, professors, and politicians are invited to participate. The debates are spontaneous, people speak fast, and the language is often very technical. If you would like to try a difficult task, check out MTV. Most of the time, you will be watching musical clips. Use closed-captioning (if available), when you try to follow the songs' lyrics: it is not unusual for many native speakers not to understand the words! The songs may be viewed as examples of modern poetry, a symbolic and often grotesque view on contemporary life.

A homework assignment

One of the most interesting ways to understand another culture is to listen to its music and songs. If you are not familiar with contemporary western rock, rap, or pop music, take a small step forward. From MTV channel, select one video clip and tape it. Sometimes MTV provides closed-captioning which will make it easy for you to write down the song's lyrics: play the tape several times, look at the screen, and copy the words. If there is no closed-captioning provided, just ask a native to help you understand and write down the words. After this, try to interpret the song: its content, any hidden context, and the expressed emotions. See what types of rhymes, allegories, and metaphors were used in this song. Remember that you don't have to like a song to analyze it.

MTV is also known for its interesting reports and a variety of discussion-based shows. The style is primarily conversational and very close to the style many students use on campus. For comparison purposes, watch movies made 40, 50, and even 60 years ago on

American Movie Classics (AMC), Turner Classic Movies, or romance classics. (Or compare to old television shows from the 1960s to the 1980s, which are featured on the Nickelodeon and TV Land channels in the evening.) Notice the conversational style in these movies and older TV shows: the words are clearly articulated and rules of grammar are carefully followed. Will you find it different from the language of the contemporary movies? (More on American movies will appear on the website.)

American Television Talk Shows

Talk shows usually feature one or occasionally two or more hosts, who chat with each other and then have conversations with invited guests. Most of these shows have a live audience, usually fewer than a few hundred people. Such shows are typically prerecorded and edited before being aired several hours later. If you take a look at the television guide you will find that major television networks offer (it depends on the day and time of the year) from four to seven daily talk shows!

With all of the available high-tech television productions, action movies, and sensational news, how is it possible for talk shows to attract their audiences and be profitable? In the age of the Internet and 24-hour news coverage, will talk shows disappear from television? To the contrary, most of the popular American talk shows not only have high ratings, but are often more popular than all the other programs offered by the network. There are several explanations for this. The shows are very personal: the language is simple—quite different from well-organized and grammatically correct sentences used by news anchors. Second, talk shows are hosted by popular individuals whose appearance becomes an event by itself. Such names as David Letterman, Jay Leno, Oprah, Jerry Springer, Montel Williams, and Jenny Jones are familiar to almost every American. Third, many of these shows feature popular guests, national and international celebrities who use this appearance as a chance to promote their new movie, book, concert tour, or album. Some talk show hosts, like Oprah or Rivera, prefer to discuss serious and sometimes dramatic issues. Others, like Leno, Letterman, and O'Donnell use a comedy-like format to entertain the guests and viewers using flashy jokes and sharp comments.

Other shows do not include such well-known guests, and follow a different entertainment format, called sensationalism, a method of selecting a bizarre, weird, or grotesque topic for its shock value and openly discussing it on the air. As a rule, people who are involved in these stories are invited to sit and talk in front of the audience. Hosts such as Leesa, Ricky Lake, and Maury Povich invite guests who might share their first sexual experiences or talk about how they hate their parents, how they love to drink blood, or run around naked. People with serious psychological problems, abused by their parents, betrayed by friends, having failed in life are frequent guests of these shows. The participants may scream and shout at each other, using profanity and throwing objects. For example, *The Jerry Springer Show*, arguably the most popular show at the end of the 1990s, was famous for frequent physical fights between the guests in front of the camera.

Many exchange students wonder about people who become guests of these shows: how could one agree to share his or her intimate and embarrassing secrets in front of an audience of millions? There is no definitive answer to this question. Keep in mind, though, that there are many individuals who dream about being on national television and would use almost anything to get their "five minutes of fame." Also, some Americans are socialized by parents, other adults, and the media to be "themselves" and not to be ashamed of who they are and what is happening to them. For some, this personal sense of independence is part of their identity. Not every person, of course, accepts this psychology, but some do and feel absolutely fine telling everybody their deepest secrets.

Many Americans have a very low opinion of some of the scandal-filled talk shows and never watch them. So when you see what is happening on the Jenny Jones or Jerry Springer shows, do not think that everyone agrees with the nature or content of these shows. If you want to skip these and other similar programs, or if you do not have much time, try to watch a program called *Talk Soup* on the E! (Entertainment) channel. It features brief and sarcastic weekly reviews of many talk shows, and runs the most interesting and bizarre episodes.

Television Dramas and Sitcoms

Television dramas and sitcoms together make up more than half of the programming featured by major networks. In general, such shows are weekly episodes staged and recorded in advance (if the show is not new, it may appear daily). Dramas usually feature plots of a serious nature, whereas sitcom is comedy (literally, it is called a "situation comedy"). You will have your personal preferences and tastes so it is impossible to give you advice about what to watch.

For educational purposes, however, take a look at several of the most popular shows, which at different times have received top popularity ratings. Note how different these shows are. Compare, for example, *Seinfeld* with *Friends*, two urban sitcoms taking place in New York. Then compare *Rosanne* to *Ally McBeal*, shows that feature contemporary American women, very different from each other. Contrast *Home Improvement* and *Married With Children*, and see how unlike American families can be. Cartoons are supposed to be for children, but you should examine and compare *King of the Hill* and *The Simpsons*, cartoon shows that feature fairly mature topics filled with sarcasm. In order to recall what you watch, use the following observation list for your comparisons:

TV Show Observation List

- Describe the main character or characters, supporting characters, place or places where major events unfold. Write down the network or channel.

- Describe a personal profile of the major character or characters (age, occupation, major interests in life, and some psychological characteristics).

- Depict what kinds of problems the main characters face and what decisions they use to solve the problems. Of course, they face different problems and use a variety of solutions, however, you are interested in finding a common pattern in their behavior. Do you find anything typically "American" in their behavior?

- For comparison purposes, try to find any similarities and differences between the main character of the show and some popular television or literary characters from your home country (if the comparison is possible, of course).

Politics on Television

In addition to the textbook and lectures, you can get a lot of information about American politics and public life by pushing the power button on your television remote control. Remember that American politics depicted on television is not a precise reflection of contemporary American life. You cannot make generalizations about the entire society simply by watching news and politics that are covered on television. But you may learn something about the country and its political and cultural traditions. Television stations and networks compete for the viewer like you. They want you to watch *their* news and not the news broadcast of their competitors. One of the most successful ways this business does that is by bringing you the news earlier than other companies do, or by providing you with more details about the events. Therefore, American coverage of local, national, and international events is based on sensationalism, a desire to bring the first so-called "breaking news" to your home. An old journalist joke goes: "If a dog bites a man it's not news. If a man bites a dog, that's news!" Not surprisingly, you may expect that a mayor's speech during a new park opening would not attract many viewers, whereas a serious car accident would.

American television offers two versions of news: local and network news. Local news covers events close to your home. They usually feature so-called eyewitness reports and interviews about regional events: fires, injuries, local exhibitions, local weather, sports, and so on. Occasionally, some experts are invited to do analyses of the stories, but it is less common than direct coverage of events from the locations where events happen or from "beats," the locations where something is expected to occur. Watching local news can provide you with interesting stories and useful examples for class discussions and papers.

Network news is usually shorter than local news and designed to fit into a standard 30-minute format. The focus of prime-time network news is national and international: conflicts, elections, natural disasters, political statements, negotiations, and other major developments. All networks provide evening analytical programs, such as *20/20*, *60 Minutes*, *Rivera Live*, and other programs dealing with issues of public concern. Usually those reporters who are assigned to host the news or analytical programs gain national recognition and become celebrities. For example, in the 1990s, three names were generally associated with the three major networks: Dan Rather (CBS), Tom Brokaw (NBC), and Peter Jennings (ABC). When you compare the personal styles of broadcasting of these popular personalities, you might find Tom Brokaw's style calm, relaxed, and somewhat easygoing. Dan Rather might appear more active, direct, and straightforward. Peter Jennings probably has the most professional voice in the business. His style combines both his classy manners and dress code.

Also try to watch Barbara Walters (20/20, ABC) and Larry King (CNN). Americans have known Barbara Walters since the 1970s when she became the first woman to anchor the network nightly news. She is usually assigned to interview the world's most renowned politicians and celebrities. In her national program, she continues to cover controversial topics and unresolved conflicts. She is readily recognized by practically every American and also teased by many, including herself, for her inability to pronounce "r"s and for her Boston accent.

Larry King is also recognizable in almost every American home. His voice is dramatic and his sentences are short. His physical stamina and wide range of knowledge makes him a great communicator. His show features famous politicians, including former presidents, presidential candidates, and other people who have made or could make history.

Analysis of the News

If you are looking for detailed analyses of American public life and international developments, you have to watch special programs designed for these purposes. One of the oldest and highly regarded political talk shows is *Meet the Press*. This is a one-hour program aired every Sunday morning on NBC. The format of the show consists of two or three interview segments with guests of national or international importance (public officials, political leaders, and journalists) followed by a discussion at the end of each segment. Like most political talk shows, *Meet the Press* invites people of different political affiliations and ideologies. Host Tim Russert allows his guests to say as much as they want without confronting them. However, at the end of the show, he always expresses his point of view, which is usually critical. If you want to follow serious discussions and do not need to be entertained, you will definitely enjoy this show, and may learn from it.

If you can stay up late, do not miss *Politically Incorrect*, a relatively new discussion show hosted by Bill Maher on ABC. Along with serious discussions about social issues, you will hear jokes, anecdotes, and sarcastic remarks about current events. This show has a live audience and you can often hear their emotional reaction. The format of this program is unusual for a political talk show. The guests, four or five people, represent different professions, political ideologies, and personal tastes. A conservative radio talk show host may sit next to a rap singer and argue with a wife of an influential and wealthy politician. People on the show very seldom become personal, and Bill Maher does a great job turning some of his guests' serious remarks into excellent jokes. This show appeals to younger audiences and is not filled with serious theoretical discussions. However, it provides an interesting glimpse into what specialists think about current social and political issues.

One of the most entertaining and enlightening political shows on American television is *Crossfire*. It is aired by CNN on weekdays and features a 30-minute emotions-filled debate and thought-provoking discussion about the most current issues. The show has two hosts who represent and vigorously defend both liberal and conservative viewpoints. The show is always unpredictable. The hosts and the guests, among whom are White House officials, Cabinet secretaries, legislators, and social activists, do not hesitate to use strong words and straightforward explanations. The topics discussed are always provocative, timely, and greatly entertaining. The analysis of the problems discussed is not very substantial, but it is compensated for by the emotional persuasiveness of the arguments.

If you are looking for less heated political discussions, watch *Capital Gang* on Sundays, and a daily show *Inside Politics*. Both programs are aired on CNN. *Capital Gang* expresses opinions of five high-energy co-hosts, who are said to be among the best journal columnists and political analysts in the United States. The discussions are always fast-paced and entertaining, but require the viewer's knowledge of contemporary politics. *Inside Politics* is educational and generally aims to pro-

A homework assignment

Choose one weekday and watch *Crossfire* on CNN. Ask somebody to tape it if you do not have a VCR. You may also get a copy of the most recent transcripts from the show's webpage. The show is designed in a special way. One of the hosts represents the liberal (on the left) position; the other host, actually sitting to the right of the other, represents the conservative platform (on the right). Take a piece of paper and divide it in two halves with a vertical line. Practice your note-taking skills; write down and compare the arguments of both sides: use the left half of the list for the liberal arguments and the right half for the conservative ones. Which arguments sound more compelling to you? Which arguments do you like or dislike: on the "left' or on the "right"? Is there a major difference between these two arguments? If yes, what did you notice?

vide insight on how politics works in this country. Analyzing the day's events, the reporting team often tries to apprise events behind the headlines. In every TV guide you can find the time of broadcast and network (if necessary) for many other programs, such as *NBC News, Dateline NBC, The McLaughlin Group, ABC News, Nightline, 20/20, CBS News, 60 minutes, Rivera Live, Equal Time*, and *Washington Week in Review*. This list, of course, is not comprehensive but provides a cross-section of what is available today.

As we mentioned earlier, it is always fine to tape the show that you are watching, especially when the topic or subject of the televised discussion is important to you. In many cases, you can obtain a free copy of a show transcript by downloading it from the show website. Go to the network home page and find a link to the show you are looking for. The transcripts are not displayed for a long time: usually from one to three weeks and then they are replaced by more recent transcripts.

For your history classes, do not miss the History and Discovery channels. They air a great variety of documentaries and special programs featuring people who made history in this country in the twentieth century: presidents, politicians, generals, writers, and many great individuals. Many of these programs are shown several times during the week, so look at the schedule and pick the best time.

Sports on Television and Your Education

You can watch sporting events on all major networks. In addition, local stations may broadcast the most important games of favorite local teams. Occasionally, such networks such as TNT and USA will include basketball or golf in their programming. The most prominent sports channels are ESPN (with the expanded services of ESPN-2 and ESPN-3) and HTS, which broadcast major local events. Sporting events are broadcast for pure entertainment purposes. What can one learn from watching baseball or football?

There are several ways to learn from watching American sports. First, knowledge about sports help you better understand American culture, its history, and heritage. By the end of this century, the three most popular American sports were: baseball, basketball, and football (often called in other countries "American football"). Less popular, but not less attractive, are ice hockey, soccer, and golf. There are many manuals available in bookstores that tell you about how these sports were developed and what their rules are. But surely the best source of knowledge about any of these sports might be a friend who grew up in America. Watch a couple of games with him and try to understand what you are watching. You do not have to become a sports fan, use your time wisely. For example, watching sports can enrich your vocabulary. Many words and expressions used in the game are part of American conversational vocabulary. Some people use these words more often than others but most Americans can understand them. For example, the word "touchdown" is from football where the meaning is to score six points after bringing the ball into the opponent's end zone. In conversations and printed stories, this word is often used to indicate a decisive victory, breakthrough, or defeat. Write down and remember some phrases and words you hear on sports channels. Ask for their interpretation. Try to use some of them in your daily conversations. You will see how many people around you will appreciate it.

One cannot see everything about a room by looking at a mirror's reflection of it. Indeed the media can give you only a reflection of American life. Some say the media are too sensational. Others suggest that they are intrusive and violent. Many critics insist that news and shows are centered mostly on people who are well known and, therefore, celebrities replace true heroes. You should remember that the American media, above all, is private big business. The networks, newspapers, local, and cable stations constantly compete for the viewer's attention. You may have different opinions about the mass media, but it should not prevent you from examining them and learning from them. They are a great source for developing your language skills. You can expand your vocabulary by reading the newspaper daily. You could learn the nuances of American life examining television talk shows, dramas, and sitcoms. You will learn to better navigate the maze of American public life by listening to radio talk shows. Music and sports are fun to watch, but they can also be used for educational purposes. Become an active viewer, listener, and reader. The rule is simple. Always ask yourself: "What can I learn from this?"

A homework assignment

Ask somebody who is familiar with baseball, football, and basketball to explain to you the meanings of the following expressions. "Three strikes and you're out," "seventh-inning stretch," "all bases are loaded," "a wild pitch," "a home run," "fourth down and inches," "a three-point shot," "a two-minute warning." Write down the explanations. Compose your own sentences (not related to sport) that would contain these expressions. Share what you have written with your professor or a friend who is fluent in English. Ask her to interpret these sentences. Compare their interpretations with yours.

Conclusion

As one of the authors' favorite writers, John Updike, said in one of his novels: "Black is a shade of brown. So is white if you look." Indeed, sometimes similarities and differences are not as dramatic as we believed they were. Things previously unfamiliar become recognizable. Difficult problems are solved and knots are untied.

John Foster Dulles—a famous American diplomat—once said that the measure of success is not whether you have a tough problem to deal with, but whether it's the same problem you had last year. We hope that this book will help you develop new skills, so that today's difficulties can be well handled with confidence and clarity.

We hope you now know the United States a little better, and that this book has helped you. Before you close it and go, we wish to give our last piece of advice: Please live with your eyes wide open and never lose your optimism. Follow the good examples of others. Your experience in the United States will change you and make your life better. You then can make the world better in your own way.

Your success depends on you now.

Appendices

APPENDIX 1

A Selection of Books about U.S. Colleges and Universities

Barron's Profiles of American Colleges (23rd Edition), College Division of Barron's Educational Series, 1998.

The Fiske Guide to Colleges 1999 (15th Edition), Times Books, 1998.

The Insider's Guide to the Colleges: 1999 (25th Edition), Yale Daily News.

Kaplan College Catalogue 2000, Kaplan, 1999.

Kaplan Access America's Guide to Studying in the USA, Kaplan, 1997.

The National Review College Guide: America's Top Liberal Arts Schools, Simon & Schuster Trade, 1993.

Peterson's Guides publishes about 100 guides related to colleges, including guides for specific programs of study. The following represents only a small sample of their offerings:

Peterson's College and University Almanac 1999: A Compact Guide to Higher Education, Peterson's Guides. (This includes a CD-ROM.)

Peterson's Colleges and Universities in the U.S.A.: The Complete Guide for International Students (2nd Ed.), Peterson's Guides, 1998.

Peterson's Guide to English Language Programs: World Wide English Training for Adult Learners and International Students, Peterson's Guides, 1998.

Random House publishes a very complete series of college guides under the Princeton Review Series. The following is a sample:

Princeton Review Complete Book of Colleges, Random House, 1999.

The Princeton Review International Student Handbook: A Guide to Colleges and Graduate Schools in the U.S.A., Random House, 1996.

APPENDIX 2

A Sample List of Evaluation Services

World Education Services, Inc.
P.O. Box 745
Old Chelsea Station
New York, NY 10113-0745
Phone (212) 966-6311
Fax (212) 966-6395
Email info@wes.org
Webpage: www.wes.com

World Education Credentials Evaluators
P.O. Box 726
Herndon, VA 22070
Phone (703) 689-0894
Fax (703) 707-0291
Email wecewellington@erols.com
Webpage: www.erols.com/wecewellington

Educational Credential Evaluators, Inc.
P.O. Box 92970
Milwaukee, WI 53202-0970
Phone (414) 289-3400
Fax (414) 289-3411
Email eval@ece.org
Webpage: www.ece.org

International Consultants of Delaware, Inc.
109 Barksdale Professional Center
Newark, Delaware 19711
Phone (302) 737-8715
Fax (302) 737-8756
Email icd@icdel.com

International Education Research Foundation, Inc.
P.O. Box 66940
Los Angeles, CA 90066
Phone (310) 390-6276
Fax (310) 397-7686
Email info@ierf.org
Webpage: www.ierf.org

APPENDIX 3

Region of Birth of U.S. Foreign-Born Population

Region of Birth of U.S. Foreign-Born Population: 1960 to 1990. **TABLE A.1**
(*Source:* U.S. Bureau of the Census Internet, Release date March 9, 1999)

CONTINENT	1990	1980	1970	1960
Total	19,767,316	14,079,906	9,619,302	9,738,091
Europe	4,350,403	5,149,572	5,740,891	7,256,311
Asia	4,979,037	2,539,777	824,887	490,996
Africa	363,819	199,723	80,143	35,355
Latin America	8,407,837	4,372,487	1,803,970	908,309
Oceania	104,145	77,577	41,258	34,730

Country of Birth of the Foreign-Born Population: 1960 to 1990 **TABLE A.2**
(selected countries).
(*Source:* U.S. Bureau of the Census, Internet, Release date March 9, 1999)

COUNTRY	1990	1980	1970	1960
Mexico	4,298,014	2,199,221	759,711	575,902
Philippines	912,674	501,440	184,842	104,843
Canada	744,830	842,859	812,421	952,500
Cuba	736,971	607,814	439,048	79,150
Germany	711,929	849,384	832,965	989,815
United Kingdom	640,145	669,149	686,099	833,055
Korea (North and South)	568,397	289,885	38,711	11,171
Vietnam	543,262	231,120	No data	No data
China	529,837	286,120	172,132	99,735
El Salvador	465,433	94,447	15,717	6,310
India	450,406	206,087	51,000	12,296
Poland	388,328	418,128	548,107	747,750
Dominican Republic	347,858	169,147	61,228	11,883

(continued)

TABLE A.2 Continued.

COUNTRY	1990	1980	1970	1960
Soviet Union	333,725	406,022	463,462	690,598
Japan	290,128	221,794	120,235	109,175
Colombia	286,124	143,508	63,538	12,582
Taiwan	244,102	75,353	No data	No data
Guatemala	225,739	63,073	17,356	5,381
Iran	210,941	121,505	No data	No data
Ireland	169,827	197,817	251,375	338,722
Yugoslavia	141,516	152,967	153,745	165,798
France	119,233	120,215	105,385	111,582
Israel	86,048	66,961	35,858	17,724
Spain	76,415	73,735	57,488	44,999
Egypt	66,313	43,424	20,666	8,316
Australia and New Zealand	57,682	47,533	32,388	28,035
Sweden	53,676	77,157	127,070	214,491
Nigeria	55,350	25,528	No data	No data
Turkey	55,087	51,915	48,085	52,228
Pacific Islands	46,463	30,044	8,870	6,695
Syria	36,782	22,081	14,962	16,717
Ethiopia	34,805	7,516	No data	No data
South Africa	34,707	16,103	7,667	5,394
United Arab Emirates	1,656	534	No data	No data

References

Anderson, K. 1997. Gender and public opinion. In B. Norrander & C. Wilcox (Eds.), *Understanding Public Opinion*. Washington, DC: CQ Press.

Cogan, J. 1997. Hate crimes and women's health lead agenda. *SPSSI Newsletter*, May, pp. 12–13.

Berry, M. F. & Blassingame, J. W. 1982. *Long Memory: The Black Experience in America*. New York: Oxford University Press.

Brislin, R. & Pedersen, P. 1976. *Cross-Cultural Orientation Programs*. New York: Gardner Press.

Broude, G. & Greene, S. 1976. Cross-cultural codes on twenty sexual attitudes and practices. *Ethnology, 15*: 409–429.

DeFleur, M. & Dennis, E. 1994. *Understanding Mass Communication*. Boston: Houghton Mifflin.

Diagnostic and Statistical Manual of Mental Disorders. 1994. Washington, DC: American Psychiatric Association.

Edsall, T. 1998. Candidates find virtue in chastity as an issue. *Washington Post*, September 28: A11.

Ellis, A. 1962. *Reason and Emotion in Psychotherapy*. New York: Lyle Stuart.

Erskine, H. 1971. The polls: Women's role. *Public Opinion Quarterly, 35*: 275–290.

Fast, Julius. 1970. *Body Language*. New York: Pocket Books.

FBI, 1996. *Crime in the United States, 1995*. Washington, DC: U.S. Government Printing Office.

Fiorina, M. & Peterson, M. 1998. *The New American Democracy*. Boston: Allyn and Bacon, p. 267.

Gallup, G. 1985. *The Gallup Poll: Public Opinion 1984*. Princeton: Gallup.

General Social Surveys: 1972–1996; Cumulative Codebook. Chicago: National Opinion Research Center.

Gordon, T. 1981. *Review Text in American History*. New York: AMSCO School Publications.

Gudykunst, W. & Bond, M. 1996. Intergroup relations across cultures. In J. Berry, M. Segall, C. Kagitcibasi (Eds.), *Handbook of Cross-Cultural Psychology*, Vol. 3. Boston: Allyn and Bacon, pp. 112–162.

Halonen, D. & Santrock, J. 1995. *Psychology: Contexts of Behavior*. Madison, Wisconsin: Brown & Benchmark.

Hill, J. 1997. Affirmative action: Roots to success. *Los Angeles Times*, March 13, 1997.

Jamison, K. 1993. *Touched with Fire: Manic-Depressive Illness and the Artistic Temperament*. New York: Free Press.

Kon, I. 1979. *Psychology of the Youth Age [Psychologiya Yunosheskogo Vozrasta]*. Moscow: Proscveshenie.

Levine, R. & Wolff, E. 1992. Social time: The heartbeat of culture. In Hurscheberg (Ed.), *One World, Many Cultures*. New York: Macmillan.

Levy, D. 1997. *Tools of Critical Thinking*. Boston: Allyn and Bacon.

Maley, A. 1993. Crossing the cultural rubicon. *Practical English Teaching*, June.

Pearlstein, S. 1999. Clinton offers regret for 'drunks' remark. *Washington Post*, October 9, 1999: A20.

Perls, Fritz. 1973. *The Gestalt Approach and Eyewitness to Therapy*. Palo Alto, CA: Science and Behavior Books.

Phillips, D. 1998. Is a culture a factor in air crashes? *The Washington Post*, 18 March: A17.

Phinney, J. S. 1996. When we talk about American ethnic groups, what do we mean? *American Psychologist*, 51(9), September: 918–927.

Schubert, G. 1991. *Sexual Politics and Political Feminism*. Greenwich, CT: Jai Press.

Rathus, S., Nevid, J., & Fischer-Rathus, L. 1993. *Human Sexuality in a World of Diversity*. Boston: Allyn and Bacon.

Reinish, J. 1990. *The Kinsey Institute New Report on Sex: What You Must Know to Be Sexually Literate*. New York: St. Martin's Press.

Shiraev, E. & Levy, D. 2001. *Introduction to Cross-Cultural Psychology*. Boston: Allyn and Bacon.

Shiraev, E., Danilov, S., & Le, T. 2001. *Fear of Deportation*. Lanham: Lexington Books.

Sidanius, J. & Pratto, F. 1993. Racism and support of free-market capitalism: A cross-cultural analysis. *Political Psychology*, 14(3): 381–401.

Skjele, H. 1991. The rhetoric of difference: On women's inclusion into political elites. *Politics and Society*, 19(2): 233–263.

Stein, N. & Sjostrom L. 1999. *Flirting or Hurting? A Teacher's Guide on Student-to-Student Sexual Harassment in Schools (grades 6 through 12)*. Center for Research on Women, Wellesley College, www.wellesley.edu/WCW/crw-sub.html.

Strong, B., DeVault, C., & Sayad, B. 1998. *The Marriage and Family Experience*. Belmont, CA: ITP.

Tsytsarev, S. & Grodnitsky, G. 1995. Anger and criminality. In Kassinove, H. (Ed.), *Anger Disorders*. Washington, DC: Taylor & Francis, pp. 91–108.

Williams, J. & Best, D. 1990. *Sex and Psyche: Gender and Self Viewed Cross-Culturally*. London: Sage.

Williams, J. E. & Best, D. L. 1982. *Measuring Sex Stereotypes: A Thirty-Nation Study*. Beverly Hills: Sage.

Woodwards, G. 1997. *Perspectives on American Political Media*. Boston: Allyn and Bacon.

Zaller, J. 1992. *The Nature and Origins of Mass Opinion*. New York: Cambridge University Press.

Index

(Note: Numbers in *italics* indicate boxed material, illustrations, and tables.)